P9-ASE-271

OWN IT ALL

How To Stop Waiting For Change and Start Creating It. *Because Your Life Belongs To You.*

Copyright © 2019 Andrea Isabelle Lucas

Published by Mango Publishing Group, a division of Mango Media Inc.
Cover and Layout Design: Elina Diaz

Mango is an active supporter of authors' rights to free speech and artistic expression in their books. The purpose of copyright is to encourage authors to produce exceptional works that enrich our culture and our open society. Uploading or distributing photos, scans or any content from this book without prior permission is theft of the author's intellectual property. Please honor the author's work as you would your own. Thank you in advance for respecting our author's rights.

The information from *The Four Agreements* section in chapter 6 is credited to: *The Four Agreements* ©1997, Miguel Angel Ruiz, MD. Reprinted by permission of Amber-Allen Publishing, Inc. San Rafael, CA. www.amberallen.com All rights reserved.

For permission requests, please contact the publisher at:
Mango Publishing Group
2850 Douglas Road, 2nd Floor
Coral Gables, FL 33134 USA
info@mango.bz

For special orders, quantity sales, course adoptions and corporate sales, please email the publisher at sales@mango.bz. For trade and wholesale sales, please contact Ingram Publisher Services at customer.service@ingramcontent.com or +1.800.509.4887.

Own it All: How to Stop Waiting for Change and Start Creating It. Because Your Life Belongs to You.

Library of Congress Cataloging
ISBN: (print) 978-1-63353-854-2 (ebook) 978-1-63353-855-9
Library of Congress Control Number: 2018962578
BISAC category code: BUS109000—BUSINESS & ECONOMICS / Women in Business

Printed in the United States of America

"Driven by grit and grace to empower women everywhere"
—*Forbes Magazine*

OWN IT ALL

How To Stop Waiting For Change and Start Creating It. *Because Your Life Belongs To You.*

ANDREA ISABELLE LUCAS
Founder of Barre & Soul

 mango

CORAL GABLES

Praise for *Own It All*

"Andrea Isabelle Lucas is a marvel and *Own It All* is a testament to her passion, strength, and ingenuity. The best part is: she's ready to help YOU own it all, too. Read this book and be inspired and empowered."

—**Sarah Knight**, *New York Times* bestselling author of *Get Your Sh*t Together*

"What's the biggest risk you can take today? Whatever your answer, Andrea Isabelle Lucas will ensure you say yes to it. Andrea's journey from broke and abused single mom to successful barre studio owner will inspire you, challenge you, and force you to put yourself and the goals you want to achieve back at the top of your to-do list. Whether you had a difficult childhood and are still seeking to forgive and recalibrate, are someone who came into the world with heaps of privilege and have enjoyed tremendous success in your career, or you are a woman who simultaneously feels like she has a foot in both realities, *Own It All* is one of those delicious and inspiring books you want by your side to refer back to anytime you catch yourself doubting your greatness or the opportunities before you."

—**Alexia Vernon**, women's public speaking coach and author, *Step into Your Moxie*

"Andrea is a passionate teacher of barre and life itself and her story will inspire you to attainable, real ways to own your life and your destiny."

—**Elisabeth Halfpapp** and **Fred DeVito**, Exhale Barre founders, authors of *Barre Fitness*

"This book is just *so* accessible—from the way Andrea connects her personal story to inspiring lessons learned to the worksheets that allow readers to translate her advice into actionable steps for their own goal setting—but I especially appreciated how the interviews with the diverse crew of role models, from style icon Kimmie Smith to US Congresswomen Kathlerine Clark to eighty-four-year-old fitness guru Esther Fairfax, added concrete examples of women walking the walk as proof positive that empowerment is there for the taking!"

—Jen Malone, author of *The Art of the Swap*

"Full of concrete, incredibly actionable tips for setting goals and actually achieving them, this book is a must-read for anyone who's shooting for the stars."

—Sarah Von Bargen, founder of Yes & Yes

To our future.

Table of Contents

Introduction

It was an icy, black night in January. I ran through the thick snow covering my front yard, tore across the neighbors' driveway, and pounded on their front door. I was relieved to see lights through the windows and hear the sound of a TV in their den, so I knew they were home, though I had no idea what I would say when they answered. My neighbors opened the door with curious smiles, but their expressions changed to shock when they saw my swollen face.

"Oh my God! Are you all right?"

I tried to reply as quietly as I possibly could so their kids wouldn't hear me. I didn't want them to come to the door and ask what was happening. I didn't want them to see this...situation. I knew it would terrify them.

"Please," I said. "Can you take me to the hospital?"

Ours was an affluent neighborhood where people drove luxury sedans and where kids went to private schools; a place where people smiled politely, wore cardigan sweaters, attended church, and chitchatted about golf—not the type of place where battered women bang on your door in the darkness, desperate for help. Everything about this moment felt surreal and detached, like this was a movie and I was watching a character onscreen. This couldn't really be my life. This couldn't be happening to me.

Within minutes, I was buckled into the neighbors' car. The drive to the emergency room felt like one of the longest of my life. My neighbor was so kindhearted and concerned, trying to fill the awkward silence with small talk. I replied to his questions with monosyllabic answers and nods. I could barely string two or three words together. I was so ashamed. I just wanted to evaporate. I couldn't look him in the eye. All I could think to myself was, "This is so embarrassing. What must he be thinking of me right now? My life is so completely fucked up..."

Finally, we arrived at the ER. My neighbor came inside with me. I remember bright fluorescent lights and the sterile scent of cleaning products, old magazines, and unhappy patients who looked like they'd been waiting a long, dreary time. I walked up to the front desk to speak with the triage nurse and fill out the requisite paperwork.

"What happened?" the nurse asked me.

It was a simple question, but it paralyzed me. What happened? Where was I supposed to begin? I managed to stammer out a few details.

"I was home. In the living room. My partner came home and we ended up getting in a stupid argument. He just wouldn't let it go, it kept getting more and more out of hand and then..."

My voice trailed off into silence.

"...And then he swung at you?" the nurse asked, filling in the details that I couldn't seem to say aloud.

I nodded. "Yeah."

Everything replayed in my mind. That first blow had caught me completely by surprise. He'd never struck me before. Sure, there had been some red flags about his temper, but things had never escalated like this. I would never have believed he could do something like this. After punching me full in the face once, I figured he would recoil and apologize immediately. "Oh my God, I'm so sorry. I didn't mean to..."

But that didn't happen. He didn't apologize. He didn't step back. He didn't stop.

The blows came down hard and fast, one after another. I instinctively curled into a ball on the living room floor, trying to cover my head. I thought if I just stayed perfectly still, eventually he'd stop hitting me. I could feel my cheeks swelling up, narrowing my eyes. He still wasn't stopping.

After I lost count of the blows, the horrific truth dawned on me: "If I just lie here like this, I'm going to die."

I staggered to my feet and ran from the room. He caught me halfway across the room and took me by the throat, choking me and lifting me off the floor. My survival instincts kicked in. I don't exactly know how I did it, but I managed to untangle myself from his grip and escape. Adrenaline pumped through my body, making everything feel lightning-fast and slow-motion all at once. That's how I'd made it to my neighbors' doorstep. And now...here I was.

The doctors asked me to climb onto the X-ray table. They needed to make sure my orbital bones—the bones surrounding my eye sockets—weren't broken. As they placed the heavy lead X-ray blanket over my chest and flashed the bulbs, that's when it really sank in.

"I might have a shattered skull," I thought to myself. "How is this my life?"

I felt so ashamed that I had gotten myself into this situation. I knew he was the one who had done something that was so wrong. But nonetheless, I felt exposed, embarrassed, and humiliated at the consequences of my life choices.

The doctors left to examine the X-rays, and they promised a police officer would come by soon to collect a statement from me. Nearly an hour went by. No one checked on me. I sat alone in the painfully bright examination room, left to contend with my thoughts.

"How did I get here?"

I had to admit, there had been plenty of red flags. He had trouble controlling his drinking, and he got loud and aggressive after a few cocktails. That was one of the many warning signs that I'd chosen to ignore.

He liked to be in control, and I'd willingly given control over to him. He was in charge of our finances, our social life, where we lived, and where we went. In spite of our affluent financial situation, I didn't even have my own credit card. Everything was under his management.

And of course, we fought all the time.

During one of our worst fights, he drove so aggressively that he skidded the car off the road and we smashed into a wall. Miraculously, we weren't hurt, but the car was wrecked, the airbags inflating in a jarring split second. I was terrified and embarrassed. I remember calling a girlfriend later that night, standing outside in the rain as I sobbed into the phone, explaining what had happened...hoping that she'd say the "magic words" that would give me the courage to leave him.

That's what I always did. After a really bad fight, I would call a family member, or a friend, pleading for advice. I was waiting for someone to tell me, "Andrea, you need to leave him," and, "It's OK if you don't have any money. Just go. You'll figure things out." I was waiting for someone to give me permission to walk away. But no one ever did— not even on the night I wound up in the ER; in fact, when I called my parents to tell them what had happened, my father told me, "What are you going to do? You can't leave him." True story.

I guess as far as my dad was concerned, I couldn't survive on my own, since I had no money, no college degree, and no immediate job prospects. Staying with my current partner was the only viable option, because he could support me financially. Sound crazy? Especially coming from someone's own father? Yes, it totally did sound nuts. But that's what he said. Even in the midst of my own rock-bottom moment, I knew this was beyond messed up.

After that phone call, I realized: "No one is coming to save me. Not even my family."

When you get beaten so badly that your eye socket might have been crushed, it has a funny way of shaking you awake. Sitting there in that examination room, suddenly everything became crystal clear.

"Nobody is going to fix my life for me," I said to myself. "I've got to do this myself. I don't know how, but it's got to happen. I need to take charge of my life. No matter what."

Later that night, after we got tired of waiting around at the hospital for the police to show up, my neighbor drove me over to the sheriff's office and I gave my official statement.

In the days that followed, I contacted a local support center, and they connected me with lawyers and advocates who could help me...for free, thank God. Piece by piece, we put together a plan to get me out of that relationship, out of the state, and into a new chapter of my life.

It wasn't easy. I couldn't just waltz out and get my own place. I was unemployed. My credit history was a disaster. I had no credit card, no bank account, absolutely nothing. Everything, even my cell phone plan, was in my partner's name, and he could cut me off at any time. Financially speaking, he owned me. I owned literally nothing.

And the worst part of all was that...I'd allowed this to happen. I let myself become completely dependent on him. Whatever type of woman he wanted me to be, I tried to be, even if it felt like a complete lie. Whatever he wanted to control, I let him control. He had promised me a lifetime of security and comfort. At the time, that kind of offer seemed too good to pass up. Even with his erratic temper, and the frequent fighting, I didn't think I'd be able to find anyone better than him. I never dreamed that my golden handcuffs would come along with violent consequences. I never thought it would get as bad as it did.

That night in the ER was the most horrifying experience of my entire life. But I don't regret going through that experience, because it was the wake-up call I so desperately needed. It was the night I stopped waiting for someone to rescue me. It was the night I stopped blaming other people for my own shitty choices. It was the night

I stopped thinking about myself as a helpless character in a story that somebody else was writing.

It was the night I finally took ownership of my life.

This Is Your One and Only Life

Why am I writing this book?

I'm writing this book because I want you to have the best possible life you can have.

I want you to feel healthy, confident, and strong, as every human being deserves to feel. I want you to have beautiful relationships and meaningful work that excites you. I want you to feel 100 percent self-expressed and to create a legacy that you can be proud of having shaped. Your legacy might be raising enough money to build a school for kids in Cambodia, or building your own business in America, or working to change the broken health care system, or mentoring teenagers to help them get ready for college, or running for president, or opening a kickboxing studio, or writing a book filled with stories and advice just like this one.

We're all capable of leaving a positive mark on the world. I want you to leave yours.

But in order to do that, you need to take ownership of your life. You need to get clear about what you want your legacy to be. You need to get honest about where your time is currently going, what you need to focus on every day, and what needs to get cleared out of your life in order for you to thrive.

There are probably quite a few changes you'd like to make; things you want to start doing; things you want to stop doing; standards you need to raise; tiring, draining situations that really shouldn't continue any longer.

I want you to make all of those changes, and I want you to begin that journey today.

I don't want you to wait until you hit rock bottom like me.

Don't wait, as I did, until you've been battered. Don't wait until you need emergency heart surgery, or until you're so miserable that you sink into the throes of addiction, or until you wake up one morning and admit to yourself that you've been married to the wrong person for twenty years, or until you've given three decades of your life away to a career that's not right for you.

Please don't wait that long.

This is your one and only life. The clock is ticking. This is it.

Nobody is going to improve your life for you. Nobody is going to build your legacy for you, either. If you want to feel different or to live differently, then you've got to take ownership of those goals. Nobody can make those changes except for *you*.

> *"Tell me, what is it you plan to do with your one wild and precious life?"*
>
> —Mary Oliver

What It Means to Take Ownership of Your Life

I got myself entangled in an abusive relationship. You've already read one piece of that ugly story. But I've since spent more than ten years in a loving relationship with someone who treats me with care and respect.

I was once a broke, single, teenage mom, relying on food stamps for groceries. Now I run my own business that brings in millions of dollars per year. After having two kids, I felt out of shape and uncomfortable in my own skin. This year, I posed for the cover of a magazine in a midriff-baring top. I can do push-ups, pull-ups, and perform an aerial routine on circus silks. I'm in the best shape of my life.

I still have plenty of things that I'd like to improve. Like anybody else, I have days when I want to dive headfirst into a bucket of warm chocolate chip cookies, curl up under a blanket, procrastinate, and ignore all of my responsibilities. I have days when I lose my patience and snap at my kids. I have days when I skip my yoga class even though I promised myself I'd go. But overall, when I compare my life today with how my life used to be ten years ago, it's like night and day: a complete transformation. The version of me that existed back then doesn't even feel like "me." I almost can't believe that she and I are the same person.

Not many people know all the details of my past—maybe not even my therapist. But when people find out where I've been and what I've survived, they are usually pretty curious. I've been asked, "How did you change your life so dramatically?" and, "How did you become the person you are today?" It's a long story, which is why I needed to write an entire book. But the short version of the story is...

I took ownership of my life.

When I use the phrase "taking ownership," what I mean is...

+ I stopped waiting for other people to step in and rescue me.

+ I stopped waiting for a parent, a friend, a mentor, or a fairy godmother to tell me, "Hey, you're allowed to leave that awful relationship." "It's not too late to go back to school." "You can start something new if you'd like."

+ I stopped waiting for permission.

+ I stopped labeling myself a "helpless victim" and labeling other people "villains."

+ I stopped blaming other people for my unhappiness, for my abysmal financial situation, for my overly busy schedule, or for the way I looked and felt.

+ I stopped complaining about my circumstances.

+ I started taking personal responsibility for my choices.

+ I stopped waiting for the perfect opportunity to fall from the sky and started creating opportunities.

+ I got honest with myself about what I really wanted and decided I deserved success and happiness as much as the next person.

That's how I define "taking ownership of your life." It means that you're accepting 100 percent personal responsibility for everything you want to do, have, create, and become. It means that you take full responsibility for what happens from here on out.

It's a promise you make to yourself—a promise you keep renewing and practicing, day after day, like yoga. And just like with yoga, there's no perfection, but there's continual progress. There's always another level you can master, and, even when there are setbacks and difficult lessons to learn, there's grace, beauty, and joy in the process.

Your Life Belongs to You

All the pieces of your life—the parts that you love, and the parts you don't—each hold choices for you to make. No matter how unlucky your current circumstances or how unlikely your dreams might seem, what happens next is driven by what *you choose*. Ultimately, taking ownership of your life means recognizing that you are not helpless.

Even if someone does something horrendous to you—like what I described in the first pages of this book—even then, you still get to choose how you're going to respond. Please don't get me wrong. I'm not saying abuse is right or that it's OK. I'm saying that in my experience, once we move beyond "right/wrong" and "victim/villain," we get back into the driver's seat of our lives. The less we identify as victims, the more powerful we will feel. We get to choose what we'll say, what we'll do, and where our story goes from here. We can reclaim our power. We can refuse to see ourselves as helpless.

Despite whatever social, cultural, economic, and historical factors might be stacked against you, despite the current political climate, despite everything that has happened to you in the past, you must claim ownership of your life. If you don't, who will? In doing so, you will discover how powerful you can truly be.

Right now, you might be thinking, "This sounds like a really privileged point of view, Andrea!" So I think this is a good moment to stop and talk about privilege—a hugely important cultural conversation that we're finally having—because when we are willing to acknowledge our own privilege, we can take responsibility for our role within systems that are fundamentally inequitable. If you've been reading my story and thinking, "What you overcame is nothing compared to what I'm up against!" please stay with me. I wrote this book for *you*.

I had a difficult childhood. You've already heard a little bit about my family. When I was fourteen years old, I felt so unsafe at home that I ran away. I slept in clothing donation dumpsters and crashed on strangers' couches. I skipped school for months. A lot of times, I didn't know where I would get my next meal, or my next shower, and that's just a small piece of my story.

Yet looking back now, I can see that even through the hard times, I was luckier than many, many people on this planet. I had access to things like clean drinking water and medical care; I was able to get crisis services when I needed them. I have never been persecuted for my religious beliefs, skin color, physical limitations, or sexual orientation. That's just the hand I was dealt. I don't want a high-five, nor do I want pity for any of this. Those are just my circumstances.

While many types of privilege have played a role in my story, I ask you to please not let my advantages or anyone else's disempower you by making you doubt your own potential.

If anyone had told me how big a setback teen motherhood could truly be when I became a new mom at age nineteen, who knows what kind of future I would have lived. If I'd realized how many statistical advantage points it would cost me on the great socioeconomic scoreboard, maybe I would never have powered through college and raised my son to one day go to college and pursue his dreams. (He recently started college, by the way—proud mama over here!) If I had focused on the odds that were stacked against me, I might not have believed I could overcome abuse, buy my own home, build a fulfilling career, travel around the world, or publish a book. I'm so thankful I had the naiveté to believe I could own it all.

As the second-wave feminists of the 1960s recognized, "the personal is political." I know that sometimes we focus too much on healing the individual within the existing system and not enough on dismantling the unjust systems that cause the individual to suffer in the first place. It is my hope that this book can do both: embolden you, the reader, to take ownership of all you desire in this life—so that you can be part of the solution for others still struggling. For this reason, we will spend a lot of time discussing our life legacies.

Ultimately, this book is about putting aside all the reasons you might fail. It is about making it *no matter what.* It's about beating whatever odds are stacked against you so that nothing can hold you back from succeeding—whatever success looks like for you.

> You own your choices.

> You own your body.

> You own your time.

> Your life belongs to you.

What Would You Like to Change?

If you could wave a magic wand and change something about your life or the world—anything at all, big or small—what would it be? It doesn't have to be just one thing. Let your mind run free.

Think about it. Write it down. Or discuss it with a friend. Hold these goals in your mind as you move into the rest of this book.

Whatever it is, I truly believe *you can have it.* If you want your partner to contribute more around the house...if you want an extra twenty thousand dollars in your savings account...if you want national media exposure for your nonprofit organization...if you want a three-month sabbatical to study Spanish in Barcelona...if you want to help a phenomenal woman get elected to the Senate... if you want that Senator to be *you*...whatever you want, you've got to own that dream even if you don't yet know what the steps in the process will be. It's your life. It's your work to do. Nobody can do it for you. You've got to own it all.

If you're up for the challenge, this book is your guide to owning your goals, your time, your career, and every other aspect of your life, including the legacy you want to leave behind for future generations.

Once you take ownership of your life, it changes everything. It's like having a key that can unlock any door. It's like waking up and realizing, "I've been in charge all along. For a while, I forgot. But now I remember. Whatever I want, I don't have to wait for it. *I* can create it."

Own where you are. Own where you're going. Own your deepest desires. Own your impact. Own your life. Own it all.

CHAPTER 1

Own Your Goals

Inside This Chapter

+ Why it's crucial to take the biggest risk you can stomach today (even if it's very small).

+ Why envy isn't necessarily a bad thing—and how to use envy to clarify your next set of goals.

+ Why it's important to announce your goals publicly rather than keeping them a secret.

+ How to identify counter-productive thoughts in your head (like, "I don't have what it takes") and say something new.

+ The story of how I opened the very first Barre & Soul studio and how I learned to embrace small risks, then slightly bigger risks, and then even bigger risks.

+ How to stop procrastinating and start moving your life in the direction you want (because this is your one and only life—and you don't want to miss your shot).

Take the Biggest Risk You Can Stomach Today

On a sunny spring afternoon in Boston nine years ago, if you happened to step into the Starbucks on the corner of Boylston and Berkeley Street, you would have seen a terrified-looking woman sitting in the corner pretending to drink a cup of coffee, but really just fidgeting with her clothes and staring awkwardly at her own résumé.

That was me.

I was camped out inside this coffee shop because I wanted to deliver my résumé to my (hopefully) future boss—and I wanted to do it face to face. I figured I'd make an extra good impression if I walked up to hand it to her in person instead of emailing it like everybody else. (Plus, this would spare me the agony of wondering if she'd gotten it, should she neglect to reply.) I even printed it on fancy, creamy white paper. Very profesh.

I was applying for a job at exhale (all lowercase, no uppercase E, because they're cool and stylish like that), one of the top fitness, wellness, and spa companies in the country, not to mention the home of one of the most authentic Lotte Berk-based workouts in the industry (Lotte Berk was the dancer who originally created the fitness movement now known simply as "barre"). They're known for their elegance, attention to detail, and elevated aesthetic—down to the state-of-the-art lockers in the changing rooms and the upscale products in the showers. They're like the Ritz Hotel of fitness: swanky and luxurious.

I remembered having met a few instructors from exhale back when I was working on being certified to teach barre classes. It was like meeting a group of cool, impossibly beautiful cheerleaders from a fancy private school. The exhale instructors were just so...pulled together—the top of their industry, the *crème de la crème*. Even though I was just a newbie barre instructor, I knew that one day, I wanted to be one of them.

But first, I needed to get hired.

I wore my very best (purchased on super-clearance, or else I couldn't have afforded them) pair of lululemon yoga pants (also too cool for any uppercase letters) that day, trying to look the part. There was a particular manager I wanted to meet. I knew she'd be finishing up a class in a few minutes. Yes, I'd already checked the schedule; borderline stalker behavior, I know! With a drop-in rate around twenty-five dollars, I didn't have the money to actually go and take her class, so instead I planned to march up, shake her hand, and hand over my résumé at precisely the right moment.

But first I needed to, you know, leave the Starbucks. That was proving to be more difficult than I'd imagined. I was sweating despite the frigid air conditioning, and panicky thoughts kept racing through my mind. "I'm not qualified." "I'm not a good enough instructor." "Maybe she'll be annoyed that I bothered her." "Oh my God, everything is riding on this. I need this job." "If they say no to me, *what then?*" At that time, barre had only a cult following and there were very few options for barre teachers, aside from opening a studio, which I was nowhere near ready to consider.

I was in a precarious financial situation, just barely scraping by as a part-time barre teacher at a different studio in the suburbs. To support myself and my kids as a single mom, I knew I needed a full-time job. A real job. And I knew that working at exhale would mean working with the best of the best. I sensed it could put me on the path to success. On so many levels, this would be a huge upgrade for my career.

After stewing and breathing heavily and jostling around my now-cold cup of coffee for another ten minutes or so, I finally stood up. I walked outside, made my way into exhale, plastered an "I am so confident!" smile on my face, and handed over my résumé. If this was a scene in a movie, the most over-the-top, triumphant music would have been playing, with trumpets, tubas, and swelling violins. Because for me, this was a seriously ballsy move. I felt so courageous, so proud of myself.

The manager looked surprised to see me, but friendly, and thankfully my enthusiasm seemed to pay off, because I got the job! Eventually, I was even promoted to manager, exactly the kind of advancement I had hoped for. Working at exhale was a huge professional victory for me: it opened the doors for so many things and boosted my credibility and confidence tremendously. I even became an "ambassador" for lululemon, which meant free clothes and fancy photo shoots I couldn't have afforded otherwise that helped me to gain greater exposure. All of this later paved the way for me to launch my own fitness company, Barre & Soul.

You could say it all started in that Starbucks. The turning point was the moment I decided to take a risk—the biggest risk I could possibly muster at the time, which for me, meant standing up, walking into a building, and handing over a piece of paper to a woman I didn't know. Today, I'd like to think doing that wouldn't stress me out at all—no big deal! But at that point in my life, it felt terrifying.

That's the thing about setting goals and taking risks. What feels like "a huge goal" to you might feel like "no big deal" to someone else, and vice versa. And what felt "big and scary" to you ten years ago might feel like "no sweat" today. The key is to *keep taking the biggest risk you can stand right now*, because that's the only way to keep your life moving forward from wherever you are toward bigger things. When we risk nothing, then nothing changes.

Throughout this chapter, as we discuss your personal and professional goals, I urge you to keep asking yourself, "What do I *really* want?" and, "What's the biggest risk I could handle right now—a risk that would allow me to move a little closer to my goal?" Please, please do not underestimate the power of one small step.

If you feel scared—if you get butterflies in your stomach just thinking about your next step—*good*. That's a sign that you've chosen a worthy goal. Conquering this goal will upgrade your life, for sure. It's OK to be nervous the way I was—the way I still am, all the time. Finish your coffee, stand up, and just go for it.

Don't Have Any Exciting Goals? Ask Yourself What Makes You Feel Envious

Feel like you don't have any exciting goals right now? There's nothing on your vision board? Not even a single New Year's resolution? Nothing that you're striving for? Nothing at all?

Well, let's start with this question: *What makes you feel envious?*

Do you feel envy when you see people on Instagram posting photos of their fun beachside walks, yoga classes, brunches, and adorable Boston Terriers?

Do you feel envy when your friend announces that she's taking yet another international trip with her partner while her kids are away at summer camp?

Do you feel envy when you bump into a former colleague and she mentions that she recently started her own business, or that she's written a book, or that she bought a new house, or that she's delivering a TEDx Talk next week?

Or maybe seeing a woman wearing a seriously cute outfit sends you into spirals of envy. You glance down at your frumpy sweatpants and sneakers that you don't even like, and you wonder, "Why can't I ever look like that?"

Envy has a bad reputation. We're taught that envy is an intensely negative thing—that we should suppress it, brush it aside, be ashamed of it, and certainly not talk about it publicly. But that's not how I think about envy. I think envy is an extremely valuable emotion. It's a crystal-clear signal that there's something you want. It's like a spotlight, illuminating what your next project or goal could be. Envy isn't a curse—it's a gift.

I believe the main reason icky sensations come into play when we're feeling envious of someone else is because we don't believe we have—or can have—the thing that we want. But if you can start noticing and sitting with this uncomfortable emotion rather than running away from it, you might realize that maybe you *can* have what you want after all. There's room to explore and create something amazing.

Whenever I feel envious, at first, I get a bit grouchy—hey, it's only natural. Then I pay close attention to whatever has triggered that feeling. Whether it's when I notice someone with incredible style, a woman who's running for political office, or a mogul who's absolutely dominating her industry, if I feel envious, then I tell myself, "Cool. I want whatever she's got—or something similar. How can I make that happen?"

Instead of suppressing my envy, I've learned to own it—and it's changed my life.

Write & Discuss:
Who's Got What You Want?

Who are some people who trigger feelings of envy for you? Perhaps they are friends, colleagues, relatives, celebrities, political figures, others? What do they have that you want, too?

Write down anything you can think of on your own. Or get together with a friend and discuss these questions over coffee, kombucha, rosé, or your beverage of choice. If it's helpful, you could start with a phrase like: *"I feel envy when..."* or *"I feel envious when I meet someone who..."* Social media can be a *great* place to notice your inner green-eyed monster.

Remember: you don't have to feel guilty about your feelings. Envy isn't a bad thing. It's just information. It's a request from your heart, from your soul, expressing something that you want.

_____

_____

_____

Don't Keep Your Goals a Secret. Declare What You Want to at Least One Other Person.

A moment ago, you explored a couple things that make you feel envious—things you crave; things you admire; things you're seeking; people you aspire to be like, or to be more like. Maybe some new dreams and goals are materializing in your mind. Maybe you've realized that you want to define your signature style and upgrade your wardrobe. Maybe you want a new workout routine or a new art project; more free time, fun, and adventure; or a meaningful new chapter in your career.

Personally, my goals don't feel real until I've voiced them to at least one other human being. If I tell one of my closest friends, "OK, I'm really doing this," that's when the journey officially begins. I need to make things public, because I need accountability and support from my community. I think we all do. When we keep our goals a secret, that's when they tend to shrivel up and die.

Text Your Goal to a Friend. Make It Real.

Right now, I challenge you to pick up your phone. Scroll through your contacts. Choose a supportive friend—or a couple of friends. Write a text and describe something you want to achieve or experience this year. Describe your new goal in as much detail as you can. Assign a deadline for yourself, too.

Here's an example:

> "Hi! I have an exciting new goal that I want to share. I want to write twenty new poems this year, and I want to perform one poem—live, at an open mic night—before my thirty-fifth birthday. I'm doing this. It's on. I wanted you to be the first to know."

Here's another example:

> "Hi! I have an exciting new goal that I want to share. I want to get into the best shape of my life, mentally and physically. This means going to Pilates three times a week, hiking every Sunday, and creating a plan to transition into a job that I really love. I will have an amazing new job by September 1st or sooner. I am determined. It all starts today. Yay! PS. I'm heading out for a hike tomorrow if you'd like to join me!"

And one more:

> "Hey! I've decided to volunteer for Lifeline, a suicide-prevention hotline. I've thought about doing this for years. No more procrastinating and waiting until I'm 'not so busy.' I'm starting today. I just filled out my volunteer application! It's happening! I just wanted you to know because you're my best friend and I love you. That's all."

Write your text and send it. Just like that, you've created a new goal and you've declared it publicly. That's huge. You're taking ownership of what you really want.

Next comes more work: taking action to achieve your goal even when you're scared, even when it feels risky, even when conditions aren't perfect, and even when you really want to put things off until "someday later."

Can't Move Forward? Procrastinating like Crazy? It's Time to Upgrade Your Limiting Beliefs

It's been reported that only 8 percent of people who set New Year's resolutions actually keep them. Eight out of one hundred people. That's a pretty depressing statistic.

Why is it so difficult to keep the promises that we make to ourselves?

Why is it so hard to achieve our goals—even relatively small goals, like drinking more water, or making it to yoga class two times a week?

Many of us struggle to change our lives, even when we really want to. But why is it such a struggle? So many people have wrestled with this question: yogis; monks; therapists; life coaches; neuroscientists; and...me.

Here's what I've found to be true: if you're struggling to achieve a goal, it's probably because your goal conflicts with your underlying beliefs in some way. Maybe you don't think it's possible. Maybe you've convinced yourself that you are "inadequate."

You've decided something like, "I'm not disciplined enough," "I'm not qualified enough," "I don't know how to do that," (that was my favorite excuse for a long time!) or "I don't deserve it." Because of that belief (which is probably completely false), you're struggling to move forward. You feel stuck, or you want to quit.

Case in point: during her first year at Wellesley College, Hillary Clinton became convinced that she wasn't smart enough to be there. (I know, right? Can you imagine? Hillary freaking Rodham Clinton?!) After one month of classes, Hillary called her parents and told them she was thinking about leaving college and coming home. She didn't think she could handle the demanding academic environment. She didn't think she was cut out for it. Thankfully, Hillary's mom told her to stick it out—and she did. History was forever changed by Hillary's decision to stay and continue pursuing her goal of earning a college degree.

It's difficult to imagine someone like Hillary Clinton—someone so incredibly intelligent, strong, and courageous—feeling "not smart enough." But at one point in her life, that's what she believed about herself. This anecdote proves that when a thought pops into your head—a thought like, "I'm stupid," "I'm weak," "I'm powerless," "I don't deserve to be here"—that doesn't mean that thought is actually true. It could be completely false. Not every thought that pops into your head is a fact. Many thoughts are pure fiction.

The next time you think to yourself, "I don't have what it takes," you will need to challenge that thought. Talk back to it. Argue with it. Remind yourself, "Maybe this thought is a lie!" You don't have to believe everything you say about yourself.

Your inner monologue might sound like a constant stream of ugly, damaging "fake news." If so, it's time to change the conversation.

How to Change the Conversation

Once you've identified your self-limiting thoughts and decided which new, upgraded beliefs you'd like to have in your mind instead, you need to start saying these new things out loud for others to hear. Chances are the old script will worm its way back in if you don't get other supportive people involved. It is critical that you share your new belief, goal, or commitment with at least one other person.

You might confess to a friend the limiting thoughts you've been allowing to hold you back, or you may skip that part and just declare the new actions you're committed to taking. Sharing has two amazing side effects. First, the people in your life will naturally start to echo back to you the new things you want to hear and believe, and when others believe in your goals, it emboldens you and solidifies your belief in yourself. Second, sharing your intentions creates accountability; it lights a fire under you to deliver the things you said you'd do—it would be a bit embarrassing if you did not do them!

It's easy to stay stuck in the same old patterns (like the 92 percent of people who never follow through on their New Year's resolutions) if you keep your goals inside, let negative self-talk win, and use your failure as evidence that you can never really have what you want. Sharing your goals with others really can feel like blowing your own cover, though, because you can no longer hide out. You're exposed. It can feel incredibly risky, but the rewards are huge. Speak your goal out loud. Declare what you want and what you're going to do about it. Own it.

Write & Discuss:
Challenging Negative Thoughts

Here are several statements that lots of people say out loud—or think privately—all the time. Circle any that feel familiar to you.

If you're hanging out with a friend, read these statements aloud and see which ones sound familiar.

"I don't have what it takes."

"I'm not strong enough."

"I'm not smart enough."

"I'm not disciplined enough."

"I'm not creative enough."

"If I can't do it perfectly, then what's the point?"

"It will take way too long."

"I'm not ready yet."

"I'm not qualified to voice an opinion on that."

"Other people are experts on that, but not me."

"I'm just not the type of person who could ever do that."

"I don't have enough time."

"I have plenty of time. I can do it later."

Choose one of the statements that you circled. Then, come up with a new statement where you're challenging the original statement and arguing that the opposite is true. If possible, come up with some evidence to prove your point.

Here's an example:

"I'm not smart enough."

New statement:

> "Uh, no. Actually, I'm very smart! If there's something I want to learn, I can figure it out. I've done this many times. Here's some evidence: I taught myself how to use Facebook, Twitter, and Instagram. I taught myself how to change a flat tire. I got myself through school even though it was tough. I've learned all kinds of new things, all throughout my life. I can do it again. And I will."

Here's another example:

> "If I can't do it perfectly, then what's the point?"

New statement:

> "There's no such thing as perfection. If I wait for perfection, then I'll be waiting forever. I'm not a perfect mom, but I'm a great mom. I'm not a perfect athlete, but at least I'm in the game! I won't be a perfect business owner / politician / writer / activist either, but I won't let that hold me back."

Every time you challenge a negative thought and replace it with an empowering new statement, you start to lay down a foundation of new, positive beliefs about what's possible. You can change the quality of your thoughts, just like you can change your clothes or your hair color. Every time you notice a negative thought creeping into your mind, stop, challenge that thought, and change the conversation.

Still Struggling to Move Forward with Your Goals? Try This: Turn "But" into "And"

I once attended a course where the instructor encouraged us to think of a statement that includes the word "but." For instance:

> "I want to spend the summer traveling through Europe, *but* I have three kids."

"I want to have more free time, *but* my job is so demanding."

"I want to feel confident and sexy, *but* I'm overweight."

Then the instructor told us to cross out the word "but" and replace it with "and."

"I want to spend the summer traveling through Europe, *and* I have three kids."

"I want to have more free time, *and* my job is so demanding."

"I want to feel confident and sexy, *and* I'm overweight."

Switching that one word gives the statement an entirely new feeling. Pretty amazing, right?

When you say "but," it's like hitting the delete key on your dream. The word "but" immediately creates a trapped, inflexible feeling. You're shutting out possibilities and creating barriers instead. The moment you turn "but" into "and," it changes the conversation. With that one switch, it's easier for your mind to shift into a curious, exploratory state. Instead of scoffing and saying "No way!" you start asking, "What if?" Sure, it's possible to travel with kids. People do it all the time. You can too. Yes, it's possible to change your work schedule and create more free time. And absolutely, it's possible to weigh more than you'd like and still love yourself and feel totally sexy. It's possible to do all of those things and more.

When I find myself slipping into a negative mood, or when I'm wrestling with a problem that I can't figure out how to solve, I try to insert "and" into whatever I'm saying. It's like flipping a light switch inside my mind. Try it and see for yourself.

Big, Sexy Goals = Thousands of Small, Unsexy Steps

I was once interviewed on a podcast called *Real Talk Radio* hosted by a woman named Nicole Antoinette. It's a show dedicated to honest conversations about real life—especially the difficult, messy parts that most people don't want to discuss publicly.

I immediately liked Nicole. She's a total badass—an athlete who has completed all kinds of incredible physical feats, including running two marathons back to back and solo hiking through the wilderness with a backpack, a tent, dehydrated beans, and not much else. She recently completed an 800-mile solo hike through Arizona and Utah.

One thing that Nicole always says on her show is, "Every big, sexy goal is the culmination of thousands of small, unsexy steps."

It's so true. One of the biggest goals of my life was becoming an entrepreneur and opening my fitness studio, Barre & Soul. But I didn't achieve that goal overnight. It was a gradual process filled with thousands of small, unsexy steps. And it was a process that required me to take a lot of risks—emotional risks, creative risks, and financial risks, too.

One of the first risks was signing up for a training program to become a certified barre instructor. That might seem like no big deal to some people, but for me at that point in my life, it felt like a major risk.

With my self-esteem at an all-time low, putting myself in a situation that required teaching and public speaking was more challenging than I expected. Throughout the barre training program, there was a voice in my head telling me I should just sit down and shut up. I had so many moments when I thought to myself, "What if I spend all this time getting certified, but then I suck at teaching barre? What if this is all a big waste of time? What am I even doing?!"

It didn't help that during most of the training sessions, I felt like the class dunce. All of the other teachers-in-training seemed so graceful and athletic—like every single one was a retired ballerina, gymnast, or a reincarnated swan. Meanwhile, I was grunting and sweating like an asthmatic bulldog. It was disheartening to look around the classroom and realize, "I am definitely the *worst* one here." How was I supposed to compete with these other instructors once we were all certified and teaching classes? Who'd want to come to my sad, grunty class?

But I knew that barre had already transformed my body—and my life—and I was genuinely obsessed with it. I still am. I wanted to help other women become obsessed with barre, too. So even though it felt like a big emotional and financial risk, I finished the training program, got certified, and started teaching classes. I embraced the risk—and it was one that has paid off.

Take the Next Risk...Then the Next...and the Next

Getting certified to be a barre teacher felt like a big risk for me at the time. But it was just the first stomach-churning risk in a series of risks. That's how empires get built, and it's how goals are achieved: one risk at a time.

After teaching barre for a few years, I began to feel more confident in my abilities as a teacher. I started bringing more of my personality into my classes, developing my own signature style. I had started to teach yoga, and I began to bring some of the spiritual aspects of my yoga training to my barre classes. I used each class as a chance to express a message that was close to my heart—an inspiring quote, a mantra; some type of empowering idea that I wanted to share.

This was a great creative outlet for me. But in order to change my style of teaching and use a new format, I would have to break off from my beloved mentors, Elisabeth Halfpapp and Fred DeVito of exhale, and go off on my own. I would be leaving the studio where I had grown so much to start my own business.

Would students like my new teaching style? If I showed people more of the real me, would they respond positively? I wasn't sure. But it was a risk I was willing to take. In the end, not everyone loved my style of barre, of course—but plenty of people did. I began to build a reputation in my community. One by one, the right clients found me.

At around this point in my career, I had given up my management role at exhale and was teaching my Barre & Soul Method classes at a variety of studios. I had taken a pay cut to make this change, but it felt like something I had to do for my own sense of self-expression. I started to seriously consider the idea of running my own barre and yoga studio. But owning a studio felt like a crazy, unreasonable, stomach-churning, queasy kind of risk. It was too much—too big. The thought of starting a business gave me nightmares. In my nightmares, tumbleweeds blew through an empty studio where I sat weeping at the front desk, writing out rent check after rent check, with nothing to eat but dust and shame as I slipped into financial ruin. I couldn't imagine taking on that kind of monetary risk.

The part I feared most about opening a barre and yoga studio of my own was signing a lease. It felt like such a big commitment—a legally binding, long-term arrangement for people who don't mind being tied down and who have enough money in the bank to float a few bad months, or years. At that time, signing a lease felt like signing my life away.

I wasn't ready to make that kind of leap...not yet. So, I took a different risk—the biggest one that I could stand at the time. I contacted a couple of yoga studio owners in my area, and I asked, "Could I use your studio as a home base for my barre program?"

That way, I could teach my Barre & Soul classes and begin training other teachers in my method, but without all of the financial risk that would have come along with running my own space. It was a baby step toward entrepreneurship—still a big risk, but a risk that felt tolerable.

Sometimes, Life Pushes You into the Next Risk... Faster Than You Expect

The months rolled along. My plan was going pretty well. I was teaching Barre & Soul classes in a few studios around town—doing the classes using my own signature approach and enjoying my self-employed lifestyle, without the stress of actually running my own place.

And then...an unexpected opportunity fell into my lap.

I approached another yoga studio owner to ask about bringing my Barre & Soul program to her space. She invited me out for coffee and asked if I wanted to buy her entire business.

She was moving to another state and wanted to hand things over to a new owner as soon as possible. I'd take over her lease, her client email list, mats, props—everything.

At first, my knee-jerk reaction was, "Good Lord! Seriously? Me? Own a studio? Like, *my own* studio? Like, *now*?! Ha! I am not ready for that. No." (Did I mention I can be pretty dramatic?)

Despite my initial reaction, something deep in my gut told me, "Andrea, this is the next step for you. This is the next risk you need to take. If you back away from this opportunity, you'll regret it later."

I knew if I said "Yes," this would be the biggest professional and financial risk I'd ever taken. I couldn't see how I'd be able to pull the money together. And what about getting insurance, as well as business taxes and accounting—all that stuff that I didn't know how to do? Was I really qualified for this? I had serious doubts.

I slept on it. I crunched the numbers. I gnawed on the idea for several days, feeling pressured because I knew she needed an answer quickly. I kept thinking to myself, "If I don't do this, if I watch somebody else take that yoga space instead of me, I'll feel so jealous. I'll keep kicking myself for missing this opportunity."

I mustered all of my courage, and I told her, "I'll do it. I want to buy your business."

Making It Work, No Matter What

At that point in my life, I had never had more than a couple thousand dollars in savings at any given time, so I couldn't just write the studio owner a check. Luckily, she was willing to let me make monthly installment payments on the purchase price, and judging by all the financial records she showed me, I could expect that the business would continue to be profitable and that I'd be able to make the payments. But as we worked through the paperwork and other legal details, I faced my first major challenge as a business owner—and it was a big one.

The landlord of the yoga space didn't want to transfer the lease over to me. He had other plans for his building that he'd wanted to pursue, and he flatly refused to work with us. Which meant I was now purchasing a yoga business, but with no studio space.

At that moment, the whole deal could have fallen through, but I wasn't ready to let that happen. The studio owner and I ended up agreeing on a greatly reduced price for me to purchase the business, which was now little more than a mailing list and some used props. Even though I would have to find a completely new space and sign a completely new lease, I needed to make this work. No excuses—no matter what. There was no turning back.

I set out, determined to find a home for this yoga community. Knowing what I do now about how long it typically takes to find a space and get a studio ready to open, I should never have expected everything to come together within sixty days. Once again, thank God for naiveté, because somehow, it all worked out.

But it wasn't easy. When I first went in search of a suitable space, everything was either too expensive, too small, or needed too much construction. I searched online and in newspapers, called real estate agents, and drove up and down the streets with my kids in the back seat, looking high and low. But the right space didn't appear.

Then one afternoon, I was walking into my favorite Mexican restaurant downtown when I noticed a space across the street with brown paper over the windows. A little handwritten sign in the window said "For Lease" with a phone number.

I called and the landlord met me there. I walked into the tiny space, and my heart sank. It was too small. But my partner Jason, an architectural designer, kept insisting that we could make it work. When I realized I wasn't having any luck finding something bigger, I decided that for a year, we could make the small space work. I signed the lease, we got ready, secured our occupancy permit, and managed to move in just one day past our sixty-day goal. That "too small" space has now been in use for more than five years, and it is one of Barre & Soul's most successful locations.

In order to make the down payment on the space and get it ready to open, I had to scrape up some start-up money. I was approved for a business credit card and was fortunately able to take out small loans from my partner and my mom, who were willing to dip into their savings to help me get started. If that hadn't been an option, maybe I would have begged other friends and family, held a fundraiser event, made a crowdfunding page, or sold my stuff. No matter what, I was on a mission to make it happen.

A few years after that initial success, after having opened a second studio thanks to the success of the first, it was time for yet another risk. With Barre & Soul growing rapidly, I wanted to open a third studio location. But this time, it was a much bigger studio in a much pricier neighborhood—the heart of Harvard Square in Cambridge, Massachusetts. My stomach did somersaults when I saw the monthly rent. It was so much higher than anything I'd paid before. But once again, that inner voice told me, "This is the next step. This is the next risk you need to take."

I signed my name on the dotted line at ten o'clock on a weekday morning, then I walked into the vast, empty space and jumped around, leaping for joy (and nervousness!), yet unable to fathom that this was really mine. It felt like the kind of moment you celebrate with a glass of champagne, but since it wasn't even lunchtime yet, not many places were open. Somehow, Jason and I ended up at a dim sum restaurant, toasting this new chapter over Mai Tais and egg rolls. Once again, I was embracing a new risk. Once again, I knew, "This is terrifying. And I'm in just the right place."

If You're Unwilling to Take Risks, Then You Will Not Move Forward

I've learned that no matter what kind of goal you're pursuing, in order to achieve it, you have to be willing to take a series of risks.

You have to take *emotional risks*—like making a request and potentially hearing "No," or trying a new teaching style that flops, or sharing an uncomfortable truth with your partner, colleague, or boss.

Sometimes, you have to take *creative risks*—like publishing a blog post and then getting a negative comment or no comments at all, or doing a dance class even when you're the klutziest person in the room.

And sometimes, you have to take *financial risks*—like investing in a training program or a new degree, paying for the tools or help that you need, or leasing a new office or studio space.

If you're unwilling to take risks, then you won't move forward in life. However, this doesn't mean you need to take every single risk today. You don't have to go from "zero" to "signing an epic commercial lease" overnight. You can take small risks, then slightly bigger risks, and then even bigger ones. You can get your high school diploma in risk-taking, then your BA, then your MA, and then your PhD. You can graduate upwards into bigger and bigger risks over time.

Take the biggest risk you can stomach today, even if it's "declaring a goal to one other person" or "sending one text or email to get a conversation started." If that's what it is, then that's what it is...for today. Get on it.

What's the Biggest Risk You Can Stand Taking Today?

Take it. Inch forward.

What is the next (appropriate) risk you feel capable of taking after that? Take it. That's one more inch forward. One inch closer than you were yesterday. With each successive risk that you take, your confidence will build. Over time, you'll be able to tolerate bigger, scarier risks. It's just like yoga, barre, running, or weight lifting. Over time, you get stronger. Months go by, and suddenly you're swinging a forty-pound kettle bell like it's no big deal.

If you keep inching forward, taking increasingly bigger risks, your capacity to tolerate risk will expand. Before long, you'll be amazed by what you can do.

Write & Discuss: What Level of Risk Can You Tolerate Right Now?

Your brain is a fascinating machine. When you're considering something that feels risky—like buying a raffle ticket, or buying a house, or going on a first date—your brain processes all the information in a split second. Different parts of your brain light up in response to the need to make a risky decision. Sometimes, the section of your brain that's associated with excitement might light up ("Yes! This will be fun!"); at other times, the section of your brain that's associated with anxiety may light up ("No way. Too scary").

Scientists still don't fully understand why certain people happily seek out risks, while other people avoid taking risks as much as possible. It may have something to do with your genetics, your upbringing, natural changes to the brain that occur throughout life, or all of the above.

But most scientists agree that your brain can be trained and strengthened—just like any other part of your body. It's possible to train yourself to embrace risk, and even to enjoy it instead of running away from it. You can train yourself to tolerate increasingly bigger risks over time.

Here are some questions to help you explore your goals and ambitions as well as how you react to certain types of risks. Try answering these questions in writing here in this book, or make a dinner date with a friend and discuss these questions face to face:

Describe one of your number one goals. It can be big or small, personal or professional—anything that feels important to you. (I once led a goal-coaching workshop where one participant passionately exclaimed, "I want to rock a hat!") Describe what it is and how amazing it's going to feel once it's happening or when you achieve it.

_____

_____

_____

_____

What are some things you need to do in order to achieve that goal? Make a list of action steps. Write down a number next to each step. (10 = Feels incredibly risky, OMG, I'm going to throw up. 1 = No problem, piece of cake.)

_____

_____

_____

I tested out my barre classes at existing studios with a built-in clientele (small risk) before taking over someone else's studio (bigger risk). After running that first studio for a while, I felt ready to open a second location (even bigger risk), and then a third, fourth, and fifth. Each of these was the biggest risk I could stomach at the time, until I felt ready to graduate to bigger risks. What about you?

What are some smaller risks you could take in pursuit of your goal? You may have written down a few options in your response to the previous question. Can you think of anything else? Any other micro-risks you could take to inch forward?

_____

_____

_____

_____

_____

Let's say that one day you discover that you feel ready to take a bigger type of risk—whether that's taking out a bank loan, making a change to a new career, or having an emotionally vulnerable conversation with your boss, your best friend, or your partner. If you take that big risk, what is the absolute worst thing that might happen?

_____

_____

_____

_____

_____

_____

What if your worst-case scenario actually does happen? Could you survive it? What would you do next? Could there be a silver lining? What might that be?

Nobody Can Do the Work for You

If you're serious about achieving your goals, you've got to keep marching forward even when things get difficult. You have to show up and put in the work even when conditions are not perfect, even when you're not feeling your best, even when it's foggy and rainy outside, and even when setbacks arise.

Nobody can do the work for you. Yes, you can hire a personal trainer to help you reach your fitness goals, for example, but you've still got to lift weights, run, and sweat. That's your work. Yes, you can hire an assistant to help manage your busy schedule, but you've still got to learn how to set boundaries and say "no" to commitments that aren't right for you. That's your work. There are certain types of work that you and only you must do. And sometimes, yes, it's really flippin' hard.

When I look back on the wild, stressful weeks leading up to the opening of the first Barre & Soul studio, I'm honestly not sure how we pulled it off. We tapped into unbelievable reserves of grit and grace, and somehow—with gallons of coffee, minimal sleep, and epic music playlists—we made it happen. But it required a massive amount of work, and there were so many hurdles to clear.

One of the biggest hurdles was renovating the studio and getting it ready for opening day. I was counting on my super-handy partner Jason to help make this happen, but then a couple days after I signed the lease, he found out he needed knee surgery. Just like that, he was out of commission. I didn't have the budget to hire a non-boyfriend employee. I thought to myself, "Now what?"

But then, things took a surprising twist. A woman named Sam who regularly attended my yoga classes came up to me one night after class. "I heard the news. Congratulations on getting your own studio!" she told me. Then she mentioned that she's an interior designer.

"I don't know if you'd be interested in this, but if you need some help with the new studio, I'd love to be involved," she said. "I could help you with painting, getting furniture, whatever you need. And if you don't have the budget to pay me, I'd do it in exchange for a membership at the studio."

After I picked my jaw up off the floor, I told her, "Hell yes!"

A few days after that, I found a couple family members who worked in construction who I could hire at a reasonable rate to do a few of the tasks that Jason was originally going to do. Now I had Sam, my cousin, and my uncle on board. It was still going to be tricky to get the studio ready for opening day—which was rapidly approaching—but I knew we could do it. It wasn't going to be easy to do everything while simultaneously taking care of my kids and helping Jason recover from surgery, but I was determined to make it happen. I kept telling myself, "I chose this. I signed up for this." I knew, "This is the work that needs to get done."

Sam and I pulled several late nights painting the walls, hanging shelves, installing cubbies and lockers, and drilling barres into the walls. She made some stellar playlists for those long, tiring nights, and she was the person who introduced me to the Irish singer-songwriter Hozier. Hozier has become possibly my favorite artist ever, and his music was my personal soundtrack for the next couple of years. In spite of the long hours of hard work, those are fond memories now.

We finished the studio just in the nick of time. On opening day, longtime students, curious neighbors, friends, and family flowed through the door to check out the new space. As each new face popped into the doorway, I thought to myself, "This is really happening!" The world's first Barre & Soul studio was open for business.

There were so many moments along the way when I wanted to cry, give up, take a nap, drink a large bottle of vodka, hide, or curl into a ball...you get the idea. Opening that first studio was one of the hardest things I've ever done.

But I've learned that's what it takes to achieve any kind of meaningful goal. You've got to keep showing up and putting in the work even when you don't feel like it, even when you're anxious, and even when it's not your best day. One more step forward, even when it's tough: that's the definition of *grit*.

Keep Swimming Forward

During the 2016 Olympics in Rio, a young swimmer named Yusra Mardini competed in the hundred-meter freestyle and the hundred-meter butterfly. She was then eighteen years old, and she is a Syrian refugee. When a journalist asked about her training regime, Yusra politely explained that sometimes it was difficult to practice in the swimming pool back in Syria because, you know, bombs would come and tear holes in the ceiling—that sort of thing. But that didn't stop Yusra from training and making it to the Olympics. She concluded the interview by adding, *"When you have a problem in your life, that doesn't mean you have to sit around and cry like babies or something."*

Yusra's invincible attitude is so inspiring to me. But she's not superhuman. She's a human being, just like you or me. The type of grit that Yusra has inside her heart—that ability to keep swimming forward, no matter what—is something that I believe we all have, every single one of us. We just have to dig deep and decide to use it.

Write & Discuss: You've Got More Grit Than You Think

Often, we think to ourselves, "Well, other people are strong and brave, but not me. Other people can persevere no matter what, but not me. I don't have that kind of grit. I wish I did, but I don't. I'm kind of a wimp."

But maybe that's completely untrue. Maybe you're tougher than you think.

If you reflect back on your life—all of your experiences, your struggles, your achievements—I bet you can come up with at least one situation where you demonstrated considerable grit.

Maybe you didn't think you could withstand the pain of childbirth—but you did it.

Maybe you didn't think you'd survive your first week at your new job—but you did it.

Maybe your yoga instructor said, "Just give me five more seconds in plank pose," and you cursed angrily inside your mind and didn't think you'd make it, but you did it.

Maybe in school, you didn't think you'd be able to crank out your final term paper and turn it in by the eight o'clock deadline, but you hustled and pulled an all-nighter, and miraculously, you did it.

Maybe you didn't think you could survive the agony of losing a loved one, but you made it through that dark time. You're still standing.

Just like our sheroes—women like Hillary Clinton, like Maya Angelou, like Yusra Mardini—we're all capable of digging deep, tapping into our reserves of grit and grace, and achieving more than we thought possible. But sometimes we forget that we have this ability. We forget our own strength.

Here's my assignment for you:

Write down a list of your most impressive achievements. You can call it your Grit List, your Badass Brags, your highlight reel, or your "Hell Yes! I Did That!" List.

_____

_____

_____

_____

Read back your list whenever you doubt your strength. Refresh your memory. Remind yourself, "Oh yeah. Actually, I'm strong enough to handle anything. I can achieve anything I set my mind to. This list is my evidence. I've got what it takes."

Temporary Failure—or Permanent Regret?

Just before I signed the paperwork on my first Barre & Soul studio, my mind started racing with all kinds of terrible worst-case scenarios:

"What if this is an awful mistake? What if nobody wants to sign up and my classes are empty? What if I can't ever pay back the loan I took out to finance the studio? What if I have to dig through dumpsters to find stale bread loaves to feed myself and my kids?"

All of those "What ifs?" blew into my mind like the tumbleweeds in the hauntingly empty studio of my nightmares.

I had to give myself a major pep talk—just like you might talk to a friend who's panicking before a big date, a speaking gig, or a job interview. Here's what I told myself:

"If this risk doesn't work out, then the absolute worst-case scenario is that I'll be broke—not dead; not in jail—just broke. I've been broke before, and I survived. I could survive it again if I needed to. It would suck, for sure, but it wouldn't be the end of the world. I could get through it."

I also reminded myself that if I didn't take this risk, I would always feel disappointed in myself for not trying. I would rather feel the temporary sting of failure than live with permanent regrets.

Write & Discuss:
The Worst-Case Scenario

Think about one of your current goals. If it doesn't work out, what is the absolute worst-case scenario?

_____

_____

_____

_____

_____

If you found yourself in that worst-case scenario, what might you do to start improving your situation? What would it take to get things back on track?

_____

_____

_____

_____

_____

_____

That worst-case scenario might be pretty rough. But how will you feel if you don't try at all? What would that be like?

_____

_____

_____

Imagine you just got an email from a friend who's thinking about pursuing a big, exciting goal. She's nervous. She's doubting her abilities. She's unsure if she can handle all the risk. She's feeling all kinds of emotions. She really needs a pep talk. What would you say to her? Write an encouraging message for your friend.

_____

_____

_____

_____

_____

Whatever you'd say to that friend...you guessed it...that is what you need to say to yourself.

The Right Person Is You. The Right Time Is Today.

"I'm still pretty young. I've got plenty of time."

"I'll start on Monday. OK, uh, maybe next Monday."

"There's always next summer."

"Maybe later, once life settles down a bit."

"Things are just so busy right now."

"It's not the right time."

"I can handle it later."

These phrases seem so innocent, but they're not. They're dangerous. These phrases become beliefs, and these beliefs keep us in a holding pattern—procrastinating, stalling, putting off important decisions and action steps until a later date.

I spent my twenties telling myself, "I'm still pretty young. I can do it later"—among many other excuses. But one day, I woke up and realized that I was burning through year after year of "laters." I was going to blink and be thirty, then forty, then fifty, then sixty, and beyond. I could feel time accelerating with every passing year. And meanwhile, what was I doing with my life? What was I contributing to the world? What was I building? What type of legacy was I creating? Not the one I wanted, at least not yet.

At a certain point in life—for me, it happened just before my thirtieth birthday—we have to face the uncomfortable reality that actually, no, we can't necessarily do it later. We don't have all the time in the world. We have today—and today is always the right time to move forward.

> *"The best time to plant a tree was twenty years ago.*
> *The next best time is today."*
>
> **—Chinese Proverb**

Whatever kind of tree you need to plant, don't wait. Plant it today.

Sara Mora | SaraMora.me

She Owns It: Sara Mora

Allow me to introduce you to my friend Sara Mora, a young woman who seriously owns her goals. At twenty-two years old, she is an activist and a social media influencer. She is a sought-after speaker at immigrant rights events because of her work as an extraordinarily dedicated, smart, and compassionate advocate for immigrant rights and for women. She is also the elected co-president for the Women's March Youth Empower national cohort. Her thousands of followers have been a tool for Sara to truly advocate and speak out via social media regarding the many critical issues currently being decided in the halls of government. Sara has given speeches and led marches on more than a dozen occasions across the country and has authored acclaimed opinion pieces that have shaped the debate on the DREAM Act both in New Jersey and nationally.

ANDREA. Have you ever set a goal that made you think, "Yikes. Can I really do that? Am I capable of that?" What was that goal, and what's the status now?

SARA. Yes. Honestly, I feel like a big part of what I do involves taking risks that seem to be a stretch or too much to handle. However, about two months ago after brainstorming, I concluded it was a logical time for my main online platform to turn into a call to action instead of just one of motivation/inspiration only. This would mean using every project and bit of content in a totally different way and speaking on my platform with an urgency for action versus pure enthusiasm and motivation.

I'm only two months in, so while there is *so* much developing, I was definitely able to reach my main goal of keeping my followers on board through the transition. I am still actively working on engaging people and gaining everyone's trust so as to get my audience to engage. The transition has exceeded my expectations, thankfully.

ANDREA. Do you set new goals every year, like on January 1st? Or do you set new goals every season, every month, or every week?

SARA. At one point in time I set goals every year. Now I set goals every month as I encounter new projects and my network grows.

ANDREA. Is there a big goal that's been on your mind for a while that you haven't announced publicly yet? What is it?

SARA. Yes, I want to write a book, and I am working to develop an app.

ANDREA. Imagine a woman with a huge goal who's feeling paralyzed about how to take the first steps. If you were sitting down for coffee and an encouraging chat, what would you say to her?

SARA. I would tell her to visualize what she is looking to create. After visualizing, break down the *first* step required to literally achieve the goal.

ANDREA. What would you say to someone who isn't sure what their purpose is? What's your advice for someone who wants to do meaningful work but feels a bit lost or aimless?

SARA. I have definitely felt aimless and was not sure of my purpose at seventeen, to be exact. The biggest advice is: *get moving!* Do not stay still. When you are hungry for anything, you do not stay still.

Move. Take action on the first one or two things you love to do. Find mentors via social media. Go on Eventbrite and search up events in the topics you are most interested in. Ask questions. Create, even if you are not 100 percent confident in what you create.

ANDREA. Ellen DeGeneres is building a legacy of laughter and kindness. Barack Obama's legacy is one of hope and optimism. My legacy is to inspire women to take charge of their lives, stop waiting for permission, stop waiting to be rescued, and pursue whatever they want. If you had to sum up your own legacy in a few words or sentences, how would you describe it?

SARA. I am undocumented, so my legacy is one of resilience and of exceeding expectations placed over how successful one can be based on [one's] identity, culture, and/or any limitations. [After I'm gone,] I hope they say I was a leader who created leaders and that I left open spaces for women of color, women in general, and youth to feel they can change the world too.

Own Your Goals: Review

1. What are your top three goals right now?

_____

_____

_____

_____

_____

_____

2. What are some negative thoughts that pop into your head periodically? ("I don't know how," "I'm not disciplined enough," "It's not the right time," etc.)

_____

_____

_____

_____

_____

3. When those thoughts arise, how will you challenge them? How will you change the conversation so that you can replace limiting beliefs with empowering ones?

_____

_____

_____

4. Are there areas where you feel stuck because of something you don't know? What questions, if answered, could help you get unstuck? Write them down. Who could you ask who might be able to answer them or point you toward someone who can answer them?

_____

_____

_____

_____

5. Who have you already told about your goal(s)? Who are three more people you could tell?

_____

_____

_____

_____

_____

6. What are some of the creative, emotional, and/or financial risks that you need to take in order to achieve your goals?

_____

_____

_____

_____

_____

7. What's the biggest risk you can tolerate taking right now?

_____

_____

_____

_____

_____

The Keys to Owning Your Goals

+ Embrace envy and get honest about what you really want.

+ Tell someone! Sharing is a powerful first step.

+ Rewrite your negative thoughts and replace them with positive statements—then start saying them out loud to others.

+ Determine the biggest risk you can tolerate right now that will move you toward your goal.

+ Do it! Forget "someday"—get started *now*.

CHAPTER 2

Own Your Time

Inside This Chapter

+ The exact number of minutes that you'll probably be alive.

+ How to determine where your time should be going, and where it should not be going.

+ How to start saying "no" to commitments that feel like a pointless expenditure of your time, or that feel mis-aligned with your values.

+ How to start delegating, even if it makes you uncomfortable at first.

+ The sneaky way that indecisiveness steals away your time and energy.

+ How to take responsibility for where your time is going, prioritize like a boss, and redirect your time toward the goals and experiences that really matter to you.

The Clock Is Ticking

If you're very lucky, you'll be alive for about one hundred years. That's 52,560,000 minutes.

The average human lifespan is more like seventy-five years. That's 39,420,000 minutes.

Millions of your minutes have already been used up at this point. Where are the rest of your minutes going? This can be a startling question, but it's such an important one.

At a very basic level, taking ownership of your life means taking ownership of your time. It means taking personal responsibility for where your time is going. It means spending your time intentionally, focusing on things you really want to be doing. It means cutting out distractions and pointless commitments.

Taking ownership of your time is not easy to do. It's something I still work on every day. As my kids grow older, as my business expands, as my personal priorities shift, and as new challenges arise, there's always more fine-tuning that needs to be done. Like yoga, taking ownership of your time is an ongoing practice.

We live in a society where people—particularly women—are constantly interrupted, derailed from their work, asked to do special favors, and expected to do extra chores.

We're supposed to drop everything and be available at a moment's notice if a colleague, partner, or kid needs something. We're expected to make our own needs secondary to everybody else's. Every day, in big and small ways, we're asked to give our time away: one more carpooling trip; one more errand; one more email; one more phone call to discuss tonight's dinner plans or weekend activities. Often, our knee-jerk response is, "No problem. I'll be there. Consider it done."

Year after year, all that time adds up. One day, you blow out the candles on your thirty-second or fifty-ninth or seventy-eighth birthday cake, and you wonder, "Whoa. Here I am. Where did all of that time go?" There was a point in my life when I woke up and realized, "I'm not happy with how I'm spending my time. I need to make a big change." It was an uncomfortable realization—and it all started with a pair of khaki slacks*.

*Yes, slacks. Because you need to know these weren't just your average "pants." These were straight-up "slacks."

The Story of the Khaki Slacks

During this particular era of my life, I was dating a guy who was devoutly Catholic. I was raised Catholic too, but observing all of the Catholic rituals was never that important to me. I'd always preferred to have my own personal sense of spirituality. Organized religion had never been my thing.

But Catholicism was extremely important to him, and to both of our families, so...I pretended that I was interested. I figured I could adapt. I could become the type of woman that he wanted. (Spoiler alert: this is *never* a great way to begin a new relationship!)

During the time that we were together, Catholicism consumed a huge percentage of my time and mental energy. We went to mass every week. I sent my son to Catholic school, even though it wasn't the ideal environment for him. I allowed myself to be pressured into volunteering for all kinds of Catholic school committees—like serving hot lunch in the cafeteria. Whatever the church asked me to do, I said, "No problem. I'll be there."

I want to be very clear: I'm not saying there's anything wrong with getting involved in your local church—or your local temple, mosque, meditation center, or any other spiritual center that calls to you. If going to church brings you joy, then it's absolutely something you should do. If you love it, be part of it. The problem is...I didn't love it. I didn't even like it. I wasn't genuinely interested in this particular church and its teachings. I was just desperately trying to fit in.

I wanted my boyfriend, his family, and the people in our neighborhood to think that I belonged, that I was a good mom and a good woman. I wanted to earn their admiration and respect. Participating in these activities became a daily performance that I put on, like putting on a mask. It wasn't coming from my heart. It was all for show.

Looking back now, I'd say I poured hundreds of hours of my life into church-related commitments and activities. The entire time, it didn't feel right for me. But I suppressed my feelings and kept chugging along with a fake smile on my face.

The crowning moment was the annual photo shoot. You were supposed to get dressed up in your nicest clothes and smile for a photo, which was then included in the church directory so that other people could recognize you. The plan was to have a big Catholic wedding at that church one day—you know, a wedding of which our parents would approve. So obviously, we had to do the photo shoot. It seemed nonnegotiable.

I remember getting dressed for that photo shoot. I had bought a pair of khaki pants (ahem, slacks), a powder blue sweater (a shade that totally washed out my skin tone), loafers, and a string of pearls—clothes that I thought looked "respectable."

If I just described your daily uniform, rock on with your preppy self! But to say these clothes were not "me" is an understatement. It felt like putting on a costume. In high school, my idols were Courtney Love and PJ Harvey. My teenage uniform had been Doc Martens, stripy tights, and dark lipstick. After that, I'd spent the next five years supporting myself by working at strip clubs, donning six-inch platform heels, black eyeliner, and mini-dresses every night. Now, I was so concerned about putting that version of me to rest that I was willing to play the part of someone I was not.

The entire photo shoot was completely awkward, and I hated how the photos turned out. I looked uncomfortable and rigid, like I was holding my breath or suppressing a scream. Which is exactly how I felt.

How long did it take to do that church photo shoot? Maybe it took an hour to shop for those clothes that I hated; another hour to get dressed and do my hair; another hour to drive there and back; and another hour for the actual shoot—in total, perhaps four or five hours. There it is. For that photo shoot, I spent five hours of my life doing something that was a lie. I was masquerading as somebody I wasn't, wasting my time on activities I didn't want to be doing, trying to be the person I thought I was supposed to be. It probably won't surprise you to discover…that relationship didn't work out. I know, not exactly a big shocker.

Here are my questions for you:

> What's your personal version of "the khaki slacks"?
> I know you've got one. I think everyone's got a story like that.

> When do you feel like you're putting on a costume?

> When do you feel like you're putting on an elaborate performance in an effort to earn people's respect?

> When you look at your calendar for the upcoming month, how many commitments feel meaningful, and how many trigger feelings of resentment?

Those seemingly small commitments—one more errand, a couple more emails, a project you don't really want to do—all of those choices add up. Think about five hours, multiplied over the span of a year, or over a decade. That's a monumental amount of time—time you can never get back.

Reclaiming My Time!

If you've been living in a monastery for the past couple years and you haven't peeked at the internet in a while, then please Google "Maxine Waters—Reclaiming My Time" and watch the full video. You will not regret it.

Maxine Waters serves in the US House of Representatives. She's a strong, confident woman who doesn't tolerate time-wasting or excuse-making. Not from anybody. During an important meeting involving the House Financial Services Committee. Maxine was given a very limited amount of time to hold the floor and ask her questions—and obviously, she didn't want to waste a single second.

After she asked one of her colleagues a simple question—"Why did you not respond to my letter?"—he began awkwardly hemming and hawing, clearly trying to avoid the question. After allowing him to prattle on for a few moments, Maxine interjected and said, "Reclaiming my time! Reclaiming my time!" What she meant was that she wanted her colleague's meandering, pointless comments to be stricken and not counted as part of her official time. She knew he was just wasting her precious minutes—and she wasn't having it.

The footage of Maxine calling out, "Reclaiming my time!" went viral. People around the world applauded her courage and her take-no-shit attitude. Is she too bossy? Too demanding? Rude? Nope. She's just trying to do her job and she doesn't have a moment to waste. And if someone tries to steal her time, you'd better believe she will reclaim it. (Applause!)

We should all take a cue from Auntie Maxine, as she's known by her fans. Don't allow anyone to waste your time, to steal it, or to drain it. And this starts with *you*, of course. Don't give your time away. Don't make commitments you don't want to make. Don't over-serve other people while ignoring your own needs. For chrissakes, don't wait for someone to give it back to you. *Reclaim your time!*

Where Should Your Time Be Going?

You might be thinking, "Yes! I want to reclaim my time like Auntie Maxine. I want to spend my time wisely. I want to make my time count. But I'm not sure where my time should actually be going. I have so many things going on in my life. How do I prioritize?"

I've wrestled with those questions, too. For a long time, I thought, "Well, I'm a mom, so my kids are always my top priority. If there's any time left after that, I guess that's for...my partner?" It honestly didn't occur to me that I was allowed to carve out time that's just for *me*—time for my goals; my aspirations; my legacy.

Things started shifting during my late twenties. I had enrolled in college once again (fifth time's the charm!), and I was determined to finally earn my undergraduate degree. I was working toward a BA in English, but someone had suggested that switching to women's studies might be more up my alley. It turned out my college was holding a women's studies conference, so I went to check it out. At the conference, I stepped into a breakout session entitled something like: "How to Be More Confident in Your Decisions."

I thought the title of the workshop sounded kind of fluffy, but I was going through a rocky time personally and I knew I could use an extra dose of confidence, so I decided to attend. During the workshop, the instructor—a brilliant woman named Elizabeth Johnson—urged us to write down our passions, our values, and our talents, explaining that naming these would help paint a picture of what she called our Authentic Selves. Then she posed some challenging questions:

"As you go through your daily life—school, work, parenting, volunteering, seeing friends—do you feel *passionate*? Are your *values* being honored? Are your *talents* being used?" In other words, were we living authentically?

She also asked, "What are some roles that you play that don't feel authentic? What are some situations where you feel like you're hiding your real self, masking your true feelings, or living a lie?"

This was the first time I'd ever confronted these kinds of questions. It was unsettling but also very illuminating. My mind was blown. Maybe you're the kind of person who lives in a BS-free zone, saying what you mean, meaning what you say, and generally owning your life. At that time, I was not. I felt like I had just stepped into a minefield of personal revelations that came one after another.

During that workshop, I began to see that my life up until that point had been extremely inauthentic. My passions, values, and talents weren't being honored, and they definitely weren't being represented by the things scheduled into my calendar. In fact, they weren't just unacknowledged; in some cases, they were intentionally hidden. Almost everything I did felt like a ruse, a disguise, or a way of pleasing and appeasing other people. I was so worried about being who others thought I should be. Meanwhile, the things that made me *me* were being ignored. It was not good.

I left that workshop with pages and pages of notes, epiphanies scribbled in every margin of my notebook, new plans, and new promises to myself. I had a shitload of work to do. And I decided to start right away—which meant reimagining how I spent my days.

When we change what's on our calendars, we change our lives.

Write & Discuss: Your Passions, Values, and Talents

In order to determine where your time should be going, first, it helps to understand your passions, values, and talents (another way to think of this is "self-expression"). Then, the goal is to fill your calendar with commitments that allow you to express these hallmarks of your Authentic Self instead of ignoring or suppressing them. Discuss these questions with a few friends. Write out your thoughts here.

What are your passions?

Passions are: things you could stay up all night talking about, things you love, things you're obsessed with. (Some of my passions are: gender politics, music, social justice, activism, business, goal setting, and productivity. Oh, and *Harry Potter*. In high school I was obsessed with foreign languages, but not so much anymore. Passions aren't fixed, they can change over time, so don't agonize over getting this right. It's not etched in stone.)

_____

_____

_____

_____

_____

What are your values?

Values are things that you think are really, really important, the kinds of things where you think, "If everyone believed in this and behaved accordingly, the world would be a much better place." (Some of my top values are: feminism, equality, self-expression, honest communication, and personal responsibility. Some of your values might be: courage, community, friendships, contribution, creativity, patience, or perhaps something else.)

_____

_____

_____

_____

What are your talents?

Talents could be your natural abilities, skills you've had since childhood, things for which you're gifted, or perhaps things you've spent time cultivating or ways you feel called to contribute to the world using creativity and self-expression. (Some of mine are: resourcefulness, problem-solving, design, writing, teaching, leadership, and communicating.)

_____

_____

_____

_____

_____

When you look at your calendar for the upcoming month, do you feel that your passions, values, and talents are represented? Are they being honored? Are they part of your daily life? Or are they being suppressed, ignored, and/or left out? Is there anything in your calendar that you feel is counter to your Authentic Self?

_____

_____

_____

_____

What are some changes you could make to your schedule or calendar that would feel AMAZING, i.e., freeing, liberating, honest, or more authentic? Really use your imagination here, try not to hold back.

_____

_____

_____

_____

What's one thing you've always wanted to do, try, or experience that you keep putting off? (Some possible examples could include trying aerial yoga, taking a Spanish class, learning how to self-publish a book, volunteering at the local library and reading books to kids, making homemade pasta, or attending a political rally—whatever sounds meaningful and exciting to you.)

Whatever you just wrote down, I challenge you to schedule it right now—even if you're scheduling it for a date that's six months from now. Mark it down. Get it on your calendar. Make it official. Tell someone it's happening.

There's Only One Person Who Can Transform Your To-Do List, Schedule, and Calendar...and That Person Is You

If you're waiting for somebody to give you permission to spend your time differently, you're going to be waiting forever. Nobody is coming to your rescue. Nobody is going to say, "Hey, let me handle that. You should have some extra free time..." or, "Allow me to rearrange your schedule so that you can pursue your goals." The Google Calendar Fairy is never coming. She doesn't exist. It's up to you to decide how your time is going to be spent. Yes, it's a big responsibility, but it's one you can handle—and it's exciting, too!

Taking ownership of your time is a radical, life-altering act. It changes everything.

Feel like You've Never Got Enough Time? Start Saying "No"

One of the fastest ways to take ownership of your time is to get comfortable with using the word "no." Say "no" about ten times more than you typically do, and...boom! Just like that, your schedule frees up. You feel less overwhelmed. You can breathe again. You have so much more time and energy for the priorities that really matter to you. It's like magic.

Of course, for many of us—especially women—saying "no" isn't always easy. Depending on the situation, saying "no" can feel incredibly complicated. You might worry about burning bridges and damaging important relationships. You might feel wracked with guilt. You might even feel morally obligated to say "yes," like you're some kind of heartless monster if you decline.

Here's a funny true story about women and men and how we tend to approach saying "no" in very different ways.

Once, a colleague of mine found herself in the middle of a heated discussion with a group of about ten people: nine women and one man. One woman was describing a project she'd been asked to get involved with—for no pay. She really didn't want to do it. But her friend had asked, and she couldn't figure out how to say no. It felt so awkward.

"I like being helpful. I like supporting people in my community. I always hate saying no, even when I have almost no spare time," the woman sighed.

"I never know what to say to people in that type of situation. Like, how do you say no to a friend or a family member without hurting their feelings?" another woman chimed in.

"Ugh, yes!" "I have so much trouble with that." "I never know what to say."

The discussion rolled on for ten or twenty minutes. Finally, the lone man in the room chimed in politely.

"Um, so, maybe I'm missing something, but...what is the issue here, exactly?"

Nine women stared at him in confusion.

He continued, "When I need to say no, I just...say no. That's pretty much it."

He honestly couldn't grasp what these women were so flustered about. For him—and for a lot of men, I suspect—saying "no" is simple. It's not a complicated, stressful thing. If you don't want to do something, or if you're not available, you just say "no;" and that's the end. There's no hand-wringing or moaning or tortured self-flagellation. It's no big deal. I wish more of us—especially women—would take a cue from this guy. Imagine how our schedules would open up and how our stress levels would drop!

When someone asks me for something, my knee-jerk response—like most of the women in that room—is that I want to help out. I want to say "yes." I want to be generous, helpful, and kind. I've learned that it is possible to say "no" and *also* be generous, helpful, and kind. Those things are not mutually exclusive. You can say "no" and protect your time, and *also* help people out.

If a straight-up "no" feels like it's too bold a step for right now, or if you're inclined to be extra generous, here's a magic phrase to remember: "No, but how about..." Here's how it works:

"No, but How about..."

Let's say someone from my daughter's school emails me to say, "Could you volunteer at the silent auction fundraiser? We really need a few parents to help out on Thursday night."

I could respond by saying, "I'm not available that night, so I won't be able to volunteer this time around. But I'd love to contribute in a different way. How about if I donate a pack of barre and yoga classes for the auction?"

I'm saying "no," but I'm still offering to help out—just in a different way than they initially requested. I do this all the time, and it's amazingly effective. People often get really excited about the proposed alternative.

Here's another example. Let's say a young woman here in Boston emails me to say, "I'm thinking about starting my own yoga studio like you did. I was wondering if I could take you out for coffee and pick your brain? I have so many questions I'd love to ask you."

I could respond by saying, "Hey! It's so awesome that you're interested in starting your own business. We need more female-run companies in our community and in our world. Between work and family, my schedule is really tight, so I can't meet up for coffee. But you're more than welcome to attend the next Barre & Soul event on [DATE]. It's open to the whole community. I'll be there, and it would be a great opportunity for us to chat for a few minutes. Just come up and say hi! Also, one of my favorite books on entrepreneurship is *#GIRLBOSS* by Sophia Amoruso. Definitely check that one out if you haven't read it."

I'm saying "no," but I'm still offering to chat—just in a different time and place, and in a situation that makes sense for my schedule. I'm also offering some encouragement and recommending a great book. I'm sending lots of support to this young entrepreneur—just not the exact type of support that she initially requested.

I love the "No, but how about..." approach, because it's a great way to say "no" while still leaving a positive impression, feeling like you've contributed, and hopefully brightening the other person's day. I use this approach all the time. At this point, it's practically an automatic reflex. But this isn't just for emails. You can apply this approach to any type of request, including conversations with friends and situations at home with your partner or kids.

Try saying, "No, but how about..." at least once a day. This one little phrase will free up so much time on your calendar you won't even believe it.

Flex Your "No" Muscles Ten Times This Week

Just as an experiment, see if you can say "no" ten times this week—via email, text, talking on the phone, in person, at work, at home, or anywhere at all.

Say "no" to invitations, to requests, and to situations that don't work for you anymore. Say "no" to things on your to-do list that just aren't exciting or important right now. Remember that sometimes saying "no" means setting a new policy or expectation. For example, you could say to your teenager, "I know I always wake you up for school in the morning, but I want you to start setting your alarm and waking up on your own."

Saying "no" ten times in a row might feel like a big challenge. It might trigger some intense emotions. You might start feeling like people are going to be mad at you, or feeling that people will forget about you if you decide to skip a particular activity, or maybe feeling that you'll be perceived as a "bitch." All kinds of worries may flood into your mind. Try to notice those anxieties if they arise, and then...

Say "no" anyway.

Saying "no" is just like doing a reverse push-up at barre class. The more you do it, the less awkward it feels and the stronger you become. And remember that it's completely possible to say "no" and still be generous, helpful, and kind. You can protect your time and honor your priorities while still helping people out. There's a way to achieve both.

If You Honestly Don't Care about It, Then...Fuck It!

After dating for about a year, my partner Jason and I decided to move in together. I moved into his bachelor pad condo. The décor didn't quite suit me, and every year I'd say to myself, "This year, I'm going to renovate the condo." I'd give it new paint; new furniture; a new vibe—a whole new aesthetic, a total upgrade. "This year," I thought. "Definitely."

Except it never happened. Shortly after we moved in together, I got a new job working as a manager for exhale. It was an exciting, demanding position, and I didn't have much spare time after work. I also spent a ton of time on fun hobbies like learning aerial silks, dancing in a burlesque troupe, and blogging. A few years after that, I started the process of opening my first Barre & Soul studio location, and life got busier than ever. Between my career, travels, hobbies, and my kids, I had so much to do!

Redecorating the condo never rose to the top of my priority list. The most LIBERATING moment was when I realized, "I honestly don't care!" After years of half-committing to the idea of redecorating, I finally decided, "I'm over it. I'm taking that off my to-do list. It's just not that important to me."

It felt so good to scratch "Operation Condo Revamp" off my list. I was tired of putting pressure on myself to be a domestic goddess and create a magazine-worthy home. That kind of stuff didn't really matter to me or to Jason, either, so...*fuck it.* I gave myself permission to ignore all of the house-related stuff and focus on building my business instead.

We lived in Jason's condo for eight years before eventually shifting into a new house. For all of those eight years, the paint on our walls wasn't fresh. We had a somewhat early '90s color scheme going on—it looked a little like an episode of *Friends.* Our dishes didn't match. We had cups from the thrift store, plates from our respective previous lives, and random forks and knives from IKEA, my mom's place, and who knows where else. We had a Christmas-themed welcome mat outside our front door that sat there year-round. We just never bothered to put it away.

And guess what? We were happy. It was still reasonably cute, clean, and organized. It didn't look like a perfect, jaw-dropping photo from someone's Pinterest board, but it worked for us. And the money and energy we saved went into building a thriving business (and thriving lives) from the ground up.

You Can't Have It All, but You Can Have What's Important to You

I know that so many of us women—and some men, too—put tremendous pressure on ourselves to be living a "camera ready" life in all ways and at all times, with a fit body, freshly colored hair, manicure on point; a perfect home, perfect kids, and a perfect career; hot sex every night, and a car that's freshly washed and vacuumed; not to mention homemade kombucha happily fermenting on the countertop. Then throw in daily meditation at sunrise followed by gratitude journaling, aromatherapy, and sun salutations.

Come on! *Nobody* lives that way. It's an unattainable fantasy. It's great to have high standards for yourself, and it's great to set ambitious goals, but it's equally important to recognize that you can't do—and be—everything all at once.

I don't think it's possible to *have* it all. But it's possible to *own* it all. You can own your life and your choices.

You can decide what actually matters to you and what doesn't.

You can take ownership of your time and use it where it counts.

You can take it upon yourself to make the best of your situation when circumstances aren't ideal.

You can pour your energy into the priorities that excite you—and ignore all the rest.

To this day, I refuse to get bogged down with domestic stuff. You'll almost never find me fussing over a hot stove for hours on end. It's just not my thing. Most nights, I do something super easy like grab some pre-cut veggies and a rotisserie chicken from the grocery store—boom, dinner is done, healthy and quick. I don't send out Christmas cards in December. I don't make stuff for bake sales at my kids' schools. I don't host fancy dinner parties. We entertain guests once in a while, and it's usually a pretty relaxed affair with takeout and a few friends curled up around the couch.

Maybe I'll blossom into a full-fledged domestic goddess one day... but for now? Eh; I'm good. I've got other things to do. And maybe the same is true for you. Maybe it's time to radically shorten your to-do list and clear a lot of mental clutter from your head. Maybe it's time for a...stop-doing list.

Write & Discuss:
Make a Stop-Doing List

There's a writer named Danielle LaPorte who encourages her readers to create a *stop-doing list*. This is the opposite of a to-do list. Instead of writing down everything you want to *start* doing, you write down everything you want to *stop* doing.

You can make a big list of everything you want to delete from your social calendar; every chore or home renovation project that you don't actually care about; every habit you want to stop; every hobby you won't be starting after all; and every goal you keep writing down that fails to ignite a spark of passion. Write down anything you want to clear out of your life.

I strongly encourage you to make a stop-doing list. It's such a liberating exercise!

I want to stop doing...

_____

_____

_____

_____

_____

As you make your stop-doing list, take a minute to explore each item that you write down. Have a discussion with a friend if possible. You can ask yourself questions like, "Why did I do this thing in the past? What purpose did it serve, if anything? Who told me that I had to do that? What was I trying to prove? Who was I trying to impress?" This kind of discussion can lead to some very interesting revelations and can help you avoid getting yourself into the same situation in the future.

One more tip: If you find it difficult to commit to "stop" doing something, consider making a "Someday/Maybe" list, a technique I learned from David Allen's "Getting Things Done" method. It can feel less final to say that you may still do those things someday, but still be freeing to know you're not going to do them right now.

Delegating Is Hard—and So Necessary

I've always been a fiercely independent person. My childhood was not perfect—no one's ever is—but my family definitely taught me about the importance of self-reliance, hard work, and discipline. In our household, things weren't just handed to you. We didn't have a lot of money. If you wanted something, you had to work for it.

I'm grateful for the lessons my upbringing instilled in me. But the flip side to independence is that it can be difficult to learn how to delegate. I grew up feeling like I needed to handle everything by myself, and after becoming a single mother at such a young age, taking charge felt comfortable, at least in certain areas of my life; but reassigning tasks to other people or asking for help? Not so much.

A couple years back, I signed up for a leadership program. I was getting ready to start my own business at that point, and I wanted to become a stronger leader for my team. I figured there was a lot I could learn.

The program began. We were to come up with a project that would make a positive difference in the world. We had to figure out an idea that we could realistically do in the next few months. That was the first part of the assignment. "Cool," I thought. "I can do that." For my project, I decided that I wanted to host a fundraiser event to raise money for earthquake victims. A massive quake had recently hit Haiti, and the impact had been absolutely devastating. I knew every single dollar would make a difference.

The event I envisioned was to put together a glamorous experience for women in my local community—all for a good cause. I have always felt that every woman deserves her own professional photo shoot as a way to level the playing field between her image of herself and the images she sees in magazines and advertisements every day. So, the idea was you'd sign up, and then you'd get a fun girls' night out at a salon, complete with pin-up style hair and makeup. And there'd be a fabulous photo shoot at the end. The complete bombshell experience.

I already had a salon in mind. I was so excited to get started. But then, the second part of the assignment came along: the instructor told us that we had to find someone who could run the project and appoint that person as "leader." We had to hand over the entire project to this person and let them make all the key decisions from there on out. Cue "record screech" sound effect.

What?

I did not like this part of the assignment *at all*. I was actually pissed off at the instructor about this cruel twist. I felt like I'd been tricked! The idea of finding a leader triggered so many emotions for me. Immediately, I started thinking to myself: "They won't do it right. It's going to be so annoying to hand things over. It would be way more efficient if I just did everything myself. Plus, if someone else manages this project, then they will get all the credit..." and so on, and so on.

I felt so resistant. I wanted to finish the project my own way. But of course, that was the entire point of the assignment. It was supposed to feel annoying. It was supposed to be difficult. It was supposed to illuminate the issues you have when it comes to delegating, so you can work on those issues and become a better leader.

The instructor explained, "This project is a chance for you to learn how to recruit others who might be excited about your ideas. You're going to learn how to get other people on board and learn how to delegate effectively. It's all about relinquishing personal control so that you can achieve your greater goal."

Ugh.

The instructor was making perfect sense, but still...the whole assignment felt so irritating. Nonetheless, I was determined to succeed, so I threw myself into my project with an open mind. I found a leader for my fundraiser, even though my ego didn't really want to. I enlisted volunteers who were willing to help out. I told local businesses about the event and got them excited about donating products and other prizes. I had established the overall vision for the fundraiser, but now the details and production tasks were handled by the manager and the volunteer squad. My instructor challenged me to delegate everything I possibly could. Even though it was uncomfortable, I did it.

In the end, the fundraiser was a huge success. We raised tons of money for the earthquake fund, and the ladies who attended had a total blast. Once it was over, I had to admit to myself, "I couldn't have done this all by myself."

I'd learned a life-altering lesson: if you want to make a significant impact on the world, you can't do it alone. You can't carry the full workload by yourself. You can't micromanage every detail. You have to be willing to give up some control, and you have to get other people involved, or you'll be limiting the project's potential.

I've learned that this doesn't just apply to community projects or business-related projects; this applies to every area in life—any type of goal. Even if you want to exercise more and get back into shape, if you want to travel more, or if it's your goal to make time to start painting again, it helps to get other people involved. Start delegating.

What could you reassign to somebody else? What do you need to recruit help with? What could you clear off your plate so that you've got more time and energy for the priorities that matter to you? The more I delegate—not just in my professional life, but in my personal life, too—the happier and more successful I become.

Write & Discuss:
Make a Delegation List

When I'm feeling overwhelmed and time-crunched, I like to write down *everything* that I want to accomplish or work on in the upcoming month: business-related tasks; personal stuff; errands; chores—everything. I write it all down.

Then, next to each item, I'll write down somebody else's name, like my partner, one of my kids, an employee, a friend, and so on. I keep reassigning tasks to other people until I've delegated everything I possibly can. (Every time I do this exercise, I discover that I'm able to delegate much more than I thought.)

Sometimes delegating doesn't mean relinquishing the task altogether. It might just mean asking for help or clarification so I can get unstuck on something I've been avoiding. Once I'm done, I'm left with just a small handful of things that I really need to do by myself, and everything feels much more manageable. I can breathe again.

Try this delegation exercise out for yourself. Even if you don't have employees, be creative. You've probably got a couple people in your life who can take a few things off your plate.

For example, if you've been doing more than your fair share of chores around the house, then it's totally appropriate to ask your kids, partner, or roommate to pitch in and help out more. Or you can pay your babysitter to do a few extra chores, or hire an assistant. TaskRabbit.com is a fantastic website where you can find helpers to do all kinds of things for you—organizing storage bins, running errands, cooking and cleaning, editing documents, even waiting in line for you at the post office! Hiring professional help can be more affordable than you think.

Lastly, if there's something you can't reassign right now because you need to figure it out by yourself, but you feel stuck, then write down the name of somebody you can ask for the information you need. That list item could read something like: "Talk to Mary at the accounting firm re: setting up an LLC." That way, you have a way to make progress with that step instead of stalling indefinitely.

Things I Want to Accomplish	Reassign (or Get More Info)

Just Make a Decision Already!

In Malcolm Gladwell's famous book, *Blink*, he tells the story of a study conducted back in 1995. Sheena Iyengar, a professor of business at Columbia University, did a study on decision-making. She wanted to see how people responded to having a lot of options versus just a few options.

She and her research assistants set up a sample table in an upscale grocery store. First, they offered a selection of twenty-four types of jam. People could stop by, try a few flavors, get a coupon for one dollar off a jar of jam, and then purchase the jam—or not.

Later, Professor Iyengar repeated the exact same scenario except with six types of jam instead of twenty-four. Here's what happened: on average, when confronted with twenty-four types of jam, only 3 percent of samplers actually decided to purchase a jar. However, when faced with six types of jam, 30 percent of samplers decided to purchase a jar.

Iyangar's jam experiment proves something that most of us intuitively know to be true: when you have too many options, it can feel really overwhelming. Instead of taking action, you tend to back away and do...*nothing*.

I experienced this exact type of overwhelm back when I was planning the first Barre & Soul yoga retreat. I was so excited to host a retreat, but I felt overwhelmed because we had too many options. So many beautiful locations, amazing venues, and incredible chefs...it was dizzying. Which location should we choose? Gah! (#firstworldproblems)

At first, I tried to compare every option side by side. I made lists with pro versus con columns. I Googled and read online reviews until I was cross-eyed. It was all so time-consuming, and I still couldn't make up my mind. I was in a state of Analysis Paralysis. Eventually, I realized, "This is ridiculous. I just need to pick something and run with it. Whether I choose Hawaii or Bali or the Caribbean, it's going to be a gorgeous tropical island, and it's going to be amazing. There's no 'right' choice or 'wrong' choice here. The only 'wrong' choice is wasting more time in a state of indecision."

I picked St. Croix in the US Virgin Islands and that was that. All done. I felt lighter immediately. I could move onto the next thing on my to-do list without feeling bogged down with indecision. More often than not, we invent a false dichotomy in which there is one "right choice" that we need to discover, when in fact, many options might suit us equally well.

I went through the same thing when, a few years after starting my business, I went through the same thing when, a few years after starting my business, I was finally able to go house hunting for a bigger home for my family. At first, I tried to find the perfect house that met all of my specifications—lots of character, cute and funky, the right number of bedrooms, great location, and ideally, a nice backyard. But pretty quickly, I realized, "If I try to find a match for every single piece of my criteria, I could be searching forever. I don't want to wait that long."

In the end, we picked a house that met most (but not all) of our preferences. I could have spent more time searching, sure, but ultimately I decided, "I don't want to agonize over this decision anymore. I just want to pick something and be done with it. This house is great. Let's go with it." Just like choosing a location for the retreat, it felt so good to stop waffling and comparing options and just *choose*.

Think about all those unanswered emails in your inbox; all those invitations you haven't responded to yet; that application you've been meaning to fill out; that class you might sign up for; that project you might start, or not. Do yourself a favor and just make a decision already—in or out; yes or no; blue or yellow. You could analyze the options for the rest of your life. Or you could just decide! After all, sitting on the proverbial fence is an inherently uncomfortable position!

I love the expression, "throw your hat over the wall" to describe the act of committing to something in a way that can't be undone.

Make a non-refundable deposit, for example. Take a concrete, irreversible step forward. The moment you do it, I can almost guarantee that you'll feel freer and you'll have less mental clutter rattling around inside your brain.

Also, remember that there's a difference between *settling* for an option that's really not OK (like a house that's just not "you" at all) versus *choosing* an option that's not perfect but that's good enough (like a house that meets most of your criteria, just not all of them). Don't settle for mediocrity. But don't allow yourself to research, compare, and weigh options for an indefinite amount of time, either. At a certain point, you've got to assign yourself a figure-it-out deadline, come to a decision, and be free to move ahead.

Personally, I would rather spend five minutes doing research to find something that's "good enough" than spend five hours on research so that maybe, possibly I can find something that's a little bit better. I don't have that kind of time to spare—and honestly, nobody does. We've all got bigger things to do.

Unmade decisions are like weights around your ankles. They're dragging you down. Clear them out of your life, and you'll have far more time and energy. Just decide!

Write & Discuss:
What Needs to Be Decided?

Make a list of things that have been weighing on your mind and things that you've been going back and forth about. Then make a decision. Write down what you've decided. Cross it off your list. Trust that your choice is good enough. Move on. This will feel SO GOOD.

One place to locate these unmade decisions is in your clutter— within your home, your car, your inbox, or your brain. Clutter, in its many forms, is usually a result of a decision that needs to be made.

As always, I recommend doing this list-making exercise with a friend, partner, or someone else that you love. I know that for me personally, it's always easier to get unstuck when I talk things out rather than just sitting in my head alone.

Things I Need to Make a Decision About	Decision

Write & Discuss:
Time-Stealing Activities

Unmade decisions can suck up a lot of your time and energy. But those aren't the only time thieves. Think about the last week or two of your life. What are some chores, errands, or activities that stole away an unreasonable amount of your time?

Maybe you spent six hours scrolling around on Facebook on autopilot—but it wasn't particularly inspiring or fun. Maybe you drove across town and spent two hours battling traffic so that you could exchange a pair of shoes for a different size, and when you got there, the store was closed or they didn't even have the ones you wanted.

Write down some time-stealing activities that you want to avoid in the future, stop doing entirely, or delegate—anything that feels unnecessary, boring, annoying, or like a pointless expenditure of your time. Promise yourself: *Enough of this! Never again!*

_____

_____

_____

_____

_____

_____

_____

_____

_____

_____

Write & Discuss:
A Whole Day for Yourself

Imagine that you've rearranged your life so that you've got a whole extra day of free time. Every single week, a whole day to do whatever you want. You could study a foreign language. You could work outside in your garden. You could learn to play the guitar. You could start a business or a side business. You could get more involved in local or national politics. You could volunteer with a nonprofit. You could plan long hikes or day trips out of town.

What would you love to do with that time?

_____

_____

_____

_____

_____

Your Time Belongs to You

There's only one person who can change the way that your time is spent, and that person is _you_. You can do this. You can create an extra hour, an extra afternoon, or even a whole extra day filled with time just for _you_: time to rest, time to work out, or time to start a project that really matters to you.

This isn't an unattainable fantasy. It's totally within your grasp. But it's not going to happen magically. If you want more space in your life for meaningful experiences and projects, then you need to take ownership of your time and make it happen.

You might need to ask your partner for more help around the house. You might need to step down from your position as PTA president, or politely excuse yourself from your book club for the foreseeable future. You might have to say "no" a lot more than you used to—say "no" to your unreasonable boss, to your overly-demanding in-laws, and even to your kids. You might need to say "no" to responsibilities that you've dutifully carried in the past, like planning the annual fundraiser, or handling dinner prep every single night. You might need to do all of those things—and more.

Yes, it may feel uncomfortable to redesign your schedule. Yes, it may feel awkward to delegate and reassign tasks to other people, especially at first. But all of that discomfort is temporary—and the rewards are totally worth it.

Linda Sivertsen | BookMama.com

She Owns It: Linda Sivertsen

Allow me to introduce you to my friend Linda Sivertsen, author, podcaster, app creator, idea fairy, and speaker on the topic of... you guessed it...time. She's the creator of a TEDWomen talk as well as a course on Time Debt, a phenomenon she defines as "the misspending of time—either consciously or unconsciously—in ways that ultimately lead to a life half lived."

ANDREA. When did you discover the concept of time debt, and how was your life different before you made this discovery? I'm sure so many women can relate to this issue.

LINDA. I've always had a casual relationship with time, versus my father, who was in love with checking his watch and making sure we were at the airport at least two hours before a flight! Honestly, my way mostly worked for me. I'd set up my life to be self-employed, and I made my own schedule. But that was assuming life was stable. As soon as it wasn't—like when my husband unexpectedly left for another woman—and I had to do everything on my own (raise our child, pay all the bills, take care of our pack of dogs, etc.), I pulled sixty all-nighters in a year to keep from losing everything. I'd never heard of the concept of Time Debt before, but a friend was well versed. She'd been going to Debtors Anonymous meetings where she'd heard the term, and she schooled me: "Linda! You can't keep living like this. You need sleep!" When she called me a time debtor, I didn't know the term, but knew in my bones she was right.

Even though I was aware of the issue, it took a *long* time, years, to change. I had a big mess to clean up with the divorce and a pissed off kid (see divorce) and a home in foreclosure. The housing crisis had just hit, and I was one of millions who couldn't make my payments. It took a few years to get above water and then see the nuances of where I was still "wasting" time.

ANDREA. Can you walk us through a typical day (or week) in your life then as compared to now? What did you spend your time doing? What are some habits you used to waste a lot of time on that you don't do anymore?

LINDA. Daytime television. For a decade I watched *The View* and *Oprah* every day, without fail. I loved the break, the current events, the information that always seemed to come when I needed it. I justified the time spent by saying to myself, "I'm a ghostwriter. I need to know what's going on in the world. This keeps me informed so I can be a better writer for my clients." I'm not saying that my justification wasn't accurate, but I'd never take two hours out of a workday now to watch anything! Just no way. I still watch TV, but now I tape my favorite shows and watch them at the end of the day like a normal person (ha) and skip the commercials! And I don't watch anything every day.

I also talk far less often on the phone. Again, I try and keep my calls to the end of the day.

ANDREA. How did you stop doing those time-wasting activities? Did you quit, start delegating, or just decide it didn't matter? How did you go about clearing that stuff off your plate?

LINDA. It took seeing the wastefulness in an hourly tracker. My fiancé made me an Excel spreadsheet and I filled in what I was doing every fifteen minutes. That's when I thought, "Oh God. Going to

HuffingtonPost.com twelve times a day and watching all that TV is killing my productivity!" So, it was the practice of tracking, because you can't change what you're not aware of, and then the internal commitment to *stop* the madness.

Also, I stopped taking private writing clients—where I worked with only one person at a time—and started teaching writing retreats in Carmel for five people at a time. That changed everything. The beauty and camaraderie was way more fun, and I instantly felt more creatively fulfilled and tapped in. The groupthink blew my mind and made me a better, faster, more inspired writer and teacher.

ANDREA. Do you have an assistant, intern, dog sitter, or some other kind of helper? Has that been a good investment for you? What kinds of things do you delegate to them?

LINDA. I have a virtual assistant who is a whiz with tech and design. She's my everything. The kid is grown and living on his own, which has also radically freed me. He's my dog sitter when we travel, which is a godsend! When I was newly single and broke, I did hire a full-time assistant who helped me double and then triple my business—paying for herself several times over. I was scared to hire her but was smart enough to know that if I didn't get help, I was never going to get any sleep. She brought sunshine into my house every day. It was the smartest thing I ever did. She did light errands but mostly customer service with my clients and email. She helped me learn social media (she was young and dragged me into it), set up my telecourses (when I first started teaching book proposal writing), and was my right arm in setting up my writing retreats.

ANDREA. How do you organize your schedule? Do you use Google Calendar? A paper day planner? Do you write your top three priorities for each day on a Post-It note? What are your personal systems?

LINDA. iCal on my Mac and iPhone and a paper notebook. I write out my top six items each day and usually cross them off. I've learned to keep it simple; otherwise, it's way overwhelming because the items never end.

ANDREA. What would you do with an entire day of extra free time every week?

LINDA. Watch movies with my family. Read. Write. Always writing.

ANDREA. Do you think most women say "yes" to too many commitments? What's your advice on how to break out of that pattern?

LINDA. Yes. Always. Forever. It goes back to tracking your time. Once you see where it's going, you can ask yourself: is this what I REALLY want to be spending my precious hours doing? We're here for a blip. Once you figure out what you want more than anything else in the world and you plot how long that thing usually takes, saying yes to anything that doesn't line up with that and your other core values becomes too painful.

Own Your Time: Review

1. What are some of your greatest *passions* (things you love), *values* (things you feel are really important), and *talents* (areas where you shine, ways you feel called to contribute or express yourself)?

_____

_____

_____

_____

_____

2. Do you feel your passions, values, and talents are currently showing up on your calendar? Are they being honored in your day-to-day life? Or are they being suppressed, ignored, or left out?

_____

_____

_____

_____

_____

3. What are two or three things that need to be on your stop-doing or someday/maybe list?

_____

_____

_____

_____

4. What are two or three things that you need to start delegating to somebody else? (And who's it going to be?)

_____

_____

_____

_____

_____

5. What are two or three things that you need to make a decision about ASAP? (Get off that fence!)

_____

_____

_____

_____

_____

6. What are two or three things you're going to say "no" to in the future?

_____

_____

_____

_____

_____

_____

The Keys to Owning Your Time

+ Your time is precious—start treating it that way!

+ Fill your time with activities that honor your Authentic Self.

+ Only you can manage your time. If you don't like how you're spending it, start saying no.

+ Strengthen your delegation muscles, you don't have to do it all yourself.

+ Refuse to let indecision suck up your precious time and energy.

CHAPTER 3

Own Your Health

Inside This Chapter

+ Why taking care of your health is not optional.

+ How to identify your mental barriers ("I don't have time to take care of myself," "I can't afford a gym membership,") and break them down, one by one.

+ Why doing the "bare minimum" to take care of yourself is actually a great idea.

+ How to fuel yourself with good food, enjoy your meals, and maintain a healthy weight without obsessing over every calorie or carb.

+ How to identify sneaky things that are sapping your energy levels and impacting your health—like sitting too much or obsessively checking social media

+ Why it's totally possible to transform your body even if you've had kids, even if you've never been athletic before, even if you're a total beginner, even if...[insert your favorite excuse here]

No Matter Where You Are Today, You Can Transform Your Health

When my daughter Elise was born, I was twenty-six years old. But physically, mentally, and emotionally, I felt decades older. Like most parents with newborns at home, I was exhausted all the time, and getting a full night's sleep happened basically...never.

Taking care of two kids is stressful enough on its own, but on top of that, I was soon navigating a complicated breakup, getting ready to move to another state, and trying to figure out how to support myself and my kids financially. Between feeding Elise, getting her to sleep (she was colicky and cried most of the day), getting my son Roman off to school, fighting with my soon-to-be-ex-partner, packing my belongings into boxes, and job-hunting, there wasn't much time left over to take care of myself.

The stress was taking a huge toll on my health. Even though I was trying to create a better life for myself and my kids, it felt like I had an incredibly long road ahead, and it was scary to think about all the unknown variables. Would I be able to survive without my ex's financial help? Would I have to borrow money from my family? They didn't have much to spare, and it would be so embarrassing to have to ask. Would I ever feel OK again? What about my kids? Had I screwed up their lives forever? Were they going to spend their entire adulthoods in a therapist's office because of the choices I'd made?

I don't know how I would have gotten through this period without some kind of physical outlet for my stress. During my pregnancy with Elise, a barre studio had opened up in my neighborhood, and I was quick to check it out. I had tried barre at home using some Lotte Berk DVDs, and I was surprised at how rapidly I'd seen results. After my daughter was born, I felt an urge to throw myself back into the classes. I knew they would help me feel physically and mentally stronger.

After getting clearance from my doctor to resume exercise, I went in for a class. During that first class, the instructor told us to get into a plank position. That's where you're pressing your hands flat into the floor, arms straight, with your legs extended behind you, like you're about to do a push-up. I got myself into the position and my entire body started trembling. I couldn't hold the position for more than nine or ten seconds. I had to rest my knees on the floor, and even then, I was soon lying with my face to the mat, panting.

"Holy shit," I remember thinking to myself. "I'm seriously out of shape. It's worse than I thought."

Almost every movement in the class gave me that "holy shit" feeling. Some of the movements seemed physically impossible—almost superhuman; like when the instructor told us to sit on the floor with our backs flat against the wall, press up into the ballet barre with both hands, and then lift our legs off the ground. What?! How is that even possible? It seemed like a levitation trick. What kind of witchcraft was this? And yet, the instructor could do it, and lots of the other people in the class could too. So apparently, it was possible.

As I walked out of that barre class, drenched in sweat and with my legs trembling, I realized that for the last hour, I hadn't been thinking about my breakup, worrying about my shitty financial situation, or stressing about my kids' futures. That class had been so intense, it had burned all those anxious thoughts out of my mind. I had to focus so hard just to keep up that all I could think about was the next movement in the sequence. There hadn't been any room in my mind for anything else. That barre class had provided sixty minutes of relief—a temporary vacation from the stress of my life.

I wanted to feel that relief again—as soon as possible. So, I signed up for another class, and then another. Pretty soon, I was going to barre classes four to five times a week. They offered childcare at the studio, which was nothing short of life-altering. I didn't have to find a sitter for Elise, which erased one of my biggest obstacles. Every class felt like a deep, soul-strengthening therapy session. I always left feeling a little taller, a little stronger, and ready to tackle the rest of my day.

You Can't Spell "Challenge" without "Change" (OK, you definitely can. But you know what I mean.)

Even with the on-site childcare that the studio provided, it still wasn't always easy to make it to barre class four to five times a week. I was juggling work, school, two kids—my life was full to the brim. But I took ownership of my time, wrangled my schedule, and made it happen. It's amazing what's possible when you're seriously determined.

My body adapted so quickly. Within four weeks, I was noticeably stronger, and I could see a subtle difference when I looked in the mirror. With each passing week, I mastered new movements that I previously couldn't do at all. Each time that happened, I wondered, "Well, what else am I capable of doing that I didn't think I could do?"

Barre wasn't just transforming my physical body. It was transforming my beliefs about myself. I was discovering, "I can change. I can be healthier. I can become someone who is strong."

More than anything else, I loved the people I met in my new barre community. For a long time, my social circle had been restricted to my ex, his friends, and a small handful of old friends who lived out of state. I had felt isolated for so long.

But in the barre world, I met entrepreneurs, doctors, artists, community leaders, other moms, all kinds of people with exciting goals and positive attitudes. The vibe was infectious. I loved chatting with people before class and hearing about their lives and their projects. It felt great to encircle myself with new people and fresh energy, not just the insular world that had surrounded me and my ex.

After doing barre for a few years, I felt ready to branch out and challenge myself in new ways. When I met two dynamic women, Carrie Tyler and Crissy Trayner, offering training in "aerial yoga," I was intrigued. They looked so ethereal and graceful, like something out of Cirque du Soleil, as they hung from these long ribbons of fabric suspended from the ceiling. I signed up for the training. I kept my expectations very low, because I figured it was going to be outrageously difficult. But the class actually went a lot better than I expected. I was shocked by how many of the movements I could do!

Barre had given me a good baseline of physical fitness as well as tremendous core strength, which made it possible for me to do a lot of the aerial tricks. I remember thinking to myself, "I can't believe this is my real life." Not that long ago, I'd been feeling like things couldn't get much worse. But now, here I was: liberated; soaring; surrounded by amazing people; and feeling stronger every day.

The funny thing about transformation is that you don't typically notice when it's happening because the changes are gradual and incremental. Then one day, you see yourself in a new photo, or you master a pose that you couldn't do before, and you realize, "Whoa. So much has changed."

I had that experience a couple months after I started doing barre. A friend's wedding was coming up, and she asked me to be a bridesmaid. I decided to get a spray tan before the wedding as a special treat for myself. As I stepped into the spray booth, I caught sight of my body in the full-length mirror. I remember looking at my reflection and thinking, "Is that *my* butt? Is that *my* stomach? Whose body is this?" I couldn't believe what I was seeing. I looked so different!

I went home to my little apartment, closed my bedroom door, and rummaged through moving boxes to find my digital camera. This was before Instagram, when "selfie" was a word I had not yet heard. I locked the door and sheepishly took photos of myself in my bikini—the one I could have sworn I'd never want to wear again. I could see the muscle I'd gained in my abs, arms, and shoulders. Somehow, in the crazy blur of the previous couple months, I hadn't noticed the physical changes that were taking place. It was amazing.

"Damn!" I thought to myself. I looked strong.

I felt so proud of myself—not because I looked spray-tanned and fit. I mean, hey, gotta love that orange-y glow! But the real reason I felt proud of myself is because I had taken ownership of my physical fitness. All those years of neglecting my body and living in a state of panic and stress? That era was over. I'd taken ownership of my health. When you challenge your body, it changes. For months, I'd put in the work, and now, I could see and feel the results.

Reclaiming my body and developing a consistent fitness routine taught me that our bodies and minds are not made of concrete. We are malleable. We can change. Sometimes, change is scary. Sometimes your thighs tremble. Sometimes you feel like a clumsy fool. But you can do it. If you keep challenging yourself, in as little as a few months, you could be amazed by the person you've become.

Write & Discuss:
How Do You Feel?

Try answering these questions in writing, or make a date with a friend and discuss everything in person.

Do you like how you look and feel right now?

_____

_____

_____

_____

_____

In terms of your health, if you could have *more*_____, what would it be? (More strength, more flexibility, more energy? What do you want?)

_____

_____

_____

_____

_____

In terms of your health, if you could have *less*_____, what would it be? (Less stress, less negativity inside your mind, less confusion about what to eat? What do you want?)

_____

_____

_____

_____

_____

What's one relatively small change to your daily routine that would have a big impact on your health and your quality of life? Could you make that change starting today?

_____

_____

_____

_____

_____

If you immediately start coming up with reasons why it's not possible to start today, notice that. What's running through your mind? Write down whatever's bubbling up, or discuss it with a friend.

_____

_____

_____

_____

_____

Taking Care of Your Health Is Not Optional

There are so many things you do without even thinking about it. You brush your teeth. You put on your shoes. You show up to work. You put dinner on the table for your kids. You treat people with decency and respect—well, most of the time, right?

Every day, and every week, there are so many things that you do almost automatically. You don't get into an intense emotional battle about it. You just do it. But then when it comes to taking care of your health, maybe it's a different story.

Millions of people feel that being healthy is overwhelming, complicated, emotionally exhausting, or completely unrealistic. I can empathize with people who are struggling with their weight, their stress levels, or with continual anxiety, because I've been there, too.

But here's the thing: taking care of yourself is not optional. As Jim Rohn says, "Take care of your body. It's the only place you have to live." You've got to decide, "This isn't optional for me. I'm taking ownership of my health." You've got to take charge, and take an active, determined approach, because nothing's going to change if you're passive and half-hearted about it.

Tragically, most people wait until they're facing a serious health crisis—a heart attack, emergency surgery, cancer, diabetes, or exhaustion—before they start paying attention to their health. I am urging you: please don't wait that long. You don't have to ignore your health until you hit rock bottom. You can take steps to upgrade your health right now. With a little bit of effort, you can get to a place where taking care of yourself becomes automatic, just like brushing your teeth, or checking your inbox, or locking your front door. It won't always feel as hard as it feels today.

Break Down Your Barriers

As someone who works in the fitness industry, I meet a lot of people who want to work out more, who want to eat better, feel healthier, and transform their lives. I've heard all kinds of goals and aspirations. I've also heard every excuse that you can imagine.

Here are some of the most common excuses that I hear—and that I've said to myself in the past, too. These excuses are like invisible barriers that you've built up inside your own mind. It's up to you to shatter your mental barriers. You built them, and you can tear them down.

#1. "I Don't Have Time"

There's an anonymous quote that's been floating around the internet for a few years:

> *"If you don't make time for fitness now, you will have to make time for sickness later."*

It's sobering but ultimately true. You might feel like you can't possibly spare three hours a week to walk, hike, practice yoga, or do a barre class. Or you might tell yourself it's not possible to cook wholesome meals because you're just so busy. Well, what about a few years from now when you're in excruciating pain because your psoas muscle is screwed up from sitting in an office chair for too many hours a day? What about when you wind up needing to take statins to manage your cholesterol levels, and then you have to deal with insomnia, dizziness, abdominal cramping, and other fun side effects? Or when you get a serious flu and it takes you three weeks to recuperate because your immune system is so weak? Do you have time in your busy schedule for those kinds of experiences? Probably not!

Your body is not a machine. It needs sleep, fuel, and movement in order to stay well and function properly. Even if you're incredibly busy, you can carve out a little bit of time to take care of yourself. Just keep reminding yourself that this is not optional. It's mandatory.

Even Barack and Michelle Obama, Richard Branson, and Anna Wintour—some of the busiest people on earth—make time to work out every week. But it's not just presidents, CEOs, media moguls, and celebrities. I know single working moms who manage to squeeze in a barre class when their kids are at daycare. I know other moms and dads who find free online videos and exercise at home while their kids are napping. I know broke college students who do SAT tutoring for local families in exchange for a little cash so they can buy healthier food or afford a gym membership. I know other students who bike to school because it's the only way they can squeeze in some cardio. I even met a guy who, when traveling, makes sure to walk between the airport and his hotel rather than catching a shuttle or ordering an Uber so he doesn't have to go use the treadmill once he checks in! No matter how hectic your life is, there's always a way to take ownership of your health.

And lastly, taking care of yourself might not take as much time as you think. You've got 168 hours in every week. You can set aside three to five hours for physical fitness. You can set aside one hour for meditation or a massage. These are not unreasonable propositions. You can do it.

#2. "Well, Working Out Every Day Just Isn't Realistic"

Now, when did I say you have to work out seven days a week? That's right! I didn't. Three to five times a week is much more realistic for most people—and that's plenty! You can get fantastic results from three to five workouts a week.

If you've got limited time, then the key is to focus on doing the types of exercise that give you a lot of bang for your buck—or rather, for your time investment. Aim for maximum intensity in the minimum amount of time. For example, if you do a thirty-minute workout that really challenges you, that's a lot more efficient than doing a super slow, super gentle, ninety-minute workout where you're barely even breaking a sweat. And if just getting out the door to work out is the hardest part for you, consider doubling up and working out for twice as long, so that's fewer times a week you need to get yourself there.

#3. "I Can't Afford a Gym Membership"

Are you sure about that? You can get a membership at most big chain gyms—like 24 Hour Fitness—for about thirty dollars a month. That's like one dinner at a moderately priced restaurant, or one manicure. You can probably work it into your budget.

You can also ask your local gym or yoga studio if you can work or volunteer in exchange for a membership. Lots of companies are happy to work out this type of arrangement. As just one example, CorePower, one of the biggest yoga studio chains in the US, has a Studio Experience Team program. You help out around the studio for an hour and a half per week—mostly cleaning and tidying—and then you can get an unlimited yoga membership at a reduced rate.

And let's not forget the internet! Assuming you can gain access to the interwebs, if you Google the phrase "free workout I can do at home," you'll get eighty-four million search results. There are so many options these days, it's mind-boggling. Whether you follow along with an online video, hit up the gym, or pop outside to take a walk, there are so many ways to move your body while spending zero dollars.

#4: "None of My Friends Are Interested in Doing This Kind of Stuff with Me"

When you're committed to making your health a priority but your partner, family members, or friends just aren't interested, that can definitely feel discouraging. But you can't let that hold you back. You've got to press forward, with or without their support. This is your health and your life. Your BFF doesn't have to live inside your body, you do. Even if your partner rolls his or her eyes when you lace up your gym sneakers or tries to convince you to stay home instead, you've got to stay focused on the most important person in your life: *you*. (And it wouldn't hurt to have a conversation with them about being more supportive, but I digress.)

You might want to consider making some new friends. Talk to the person on the yoga mat next to you. Find out their story. Make a date to meet up for a walk sometime, or join a running, cycling, or salsa dancing group. Find new friends who love being active and who take their health seriously. Their positivity will rub off on you.

#5. "I Know All of This Stuff, and Yet I Still Can't Motivate Myself! WTF Is Wrong with Me? Maybe I'm a Hopeless Case."

You're human. You're not a robot. You have emotions, hormones, great days, tough days, peaks, and slumps. That's all normal. You don't have to be so hard on yourself. That said, I want to echo back the central message of this chapter:

Taking care of your health is not optional.

Even if you don't always feel like it, you've still got to handle it. You fill your car's tank with gas because you want to be able to drive.

You pay your phone bill because you want to call and text. You take care of your body because you want to feel great, have tons of energy, and live a long, happy life.

You may not like hearing this, but if you don't feel like working out, set your feelings aside and do it anyway. Convince yourself to just show up. It doesn't have to be the most epic performance of your life, just be willing to do something. I met a woman in her seventies who told me, "I swim laps every morning, and I've been doing it for so long that whether or not I feel like it has nothing to do with it anymore." Even more good news: your workout doesn't care about your feelings; it'll work either way! Put fitness and all other types of self-care into the nonnegotiable section of your mind instead of viewing these things as optional.

There's a meme that's been circulating around the internet for a while. It says:

"Wow, I really regret that workout," said no one ever.

Boom. You don't have to feel like going to yoga. You don't have to feel like eating a nutritious breakfast. You don't have to feel like taking a walk outside. Just go. Just get it done. Afterwards, you'll be grateful that you did.

Do the Bare Minimum

When people ask me for advice on how to get healthier, they're often surprised when I say, "Just do the bare minimum."

"Huh?" is the response I typically get.

I know. It might sound weird. In a book that's all about taking ownership of your life—and reaching your full potential—being told to do the bare minimum might seem counterintuitive. But it's actually a really good idea.

When it comes to my health—which includes mental health as well as physical health—I like to establish bare minimums of self-care that I can hit pretty easily. I've heard this same advice shared by many wise, successful people, like writer and life coach Katherine North. Bare minimums are standards that you can meet almost automatically, without a huge amount of effort. And here's my take on them: bare minimums should be treated as nonnegotiable, therefore they must be totally attainable, because once you set them, they are simply not up for debate.

Here are some of mine:

Beauty—I put on tinted sunblock, concealer (if I have any zits, which I usually do), and eyeliner or mascara every day. Even if I don't do anything else, I'm going to do these couple of things because that's the bare minimum I need to do in order to feel put together.

Nutrition—I eat something with protein at every meal, and I eat veggies every day.

Nature—I go for a walk in nature for thirty minutes at least once a week (with the exception of the really cold winter months).

Fitness—I insist on making it to yoga, barre, aerial, rowing, or some type of fun fitness class, at the very least twice a week.

Sleep—I need a minimum of seven hours per night. If I don't get it, I make sure I catch up on lost sleep within a day or two.

Connection—I insist upon connecting with a friend at least once a week for a workout class, a glass of wine, a hug, or even just a phone call.

If I meet these minimum requirements, then I look and feel pretty good. I can keep my stress levels in check, and I've got plenty of energy. Things function well. I feel healthy. I also find that once I meet the bare minimum, I usually feel so good that I'm inspired to do more. Two yoga or fitness classes might turn into four or five. A weekly thirty-minute walk might turn into a couple of weekly thirty-minute jogs, although some weeks, maybe not! The option to go above and beyond is always there for me if I want to take it—but even if I just stick with my bare minimum level of effort, I'm good.

Bare minimums rock. They're achievable and sustainable. They feel less intimidating and far more realistic than saying, "I'm going to do a boot camp workout every morning at five o'clock, seven days a week!" Yeah. That's probably not going to happen—at least, not in my world! I know that for me, doing a grueling workout seven days a week is excessive and unnecessary. I feel confident that I can achieve my health goals by doing less. I'm a firm believer in the "done is better than perfect" philosophy. The good enough workouts that I do are better than the amazing workouts that I don't do, or that I won't do.

Mental Health Matters, Too

As you're figuring out your bare minimum standards for health, it's important to consider your mental health, too. Your mental well-being matters just as much as your physical health—and both are connected in so many ways.

When you feel stressed, your body produces a hormone called cortisol, which can lead to intense cravings, especially for sugary snacks. When you cuddle with a pet, your kids, or someone else that you love, your body produces oxytocin, which counteracts stress and reduces cravings. The way you talk to yourself during stressful moments triggers the production of certain hormones and neurotransmitters, which can help you to feel either stronger or weaker, depending. A great workout will spike your dopamine levels, which can lead to a burst of creativity at work. A scary fight with your ex can wreak havoc on your immune system.

Your mind influences your body, and your body influences your mind—it's all connected. So, we can't have a conversation about owning your health without talking about mental health, too. For example, in the section where I listed my bare minimums (on the previous page), you may have noticed that I said I insist upon connecting with my friends at least once a week. For me, this kind of social interaction is truly necessary. If I skip my friend-time a couple weeks in a row, I start to feel isolated and agitated. My problems start to feel bigger than they really are. I slip into a funk.

It's not pretty. I've learned that spending time with my friends is a very powerful type of medicine.

I also know I need at least seven hours of sleep every night. This is crucial for my physical well-being as well as my mental health. It's nonnegotiable, but it wasn't always that way. In the past, I'd often stay up until one or two in the morning watching TV with my partner, even if I had to teach a barre class at six the next morning. I honestly don't know how I did it or what the hell I was thinking. I would tell myself that it only affected me upon first waking up, but the tiredness surely affected my health overall and lingered throughout the day. Most days, I felt like a hot mess!

These days, that doesn't happen anymore. If my partner wants to fall asleep on the couch in front of the TV, that's fine, he can do that. But that's not how I roll. I no longer tag along with him as though I don't have a choice. I need to be in bed at a reasonable hour, and I don't want any electronics in the bedroom. Instead of letting my bedtime be determined by default, I've taken charge of my own sleeping schedule. He can do whatever he wants, don't get me wrong. If he wants to stay up late and be a night owl or watch movies until two, cool. Meanwhile, I put myself to bed when I need to sleep, and I feel so much better because of that shift.

Changing my bedtime is a relatively small detail, all things considered, but this is what it means to take ownership of your health. You have to do what's right for *you* instead of taking a passive role and letting other people make decisions for you. My partner is responsible for his health, and I'm responsible for mine. I don't expect him to take ownership of my sleep. That's my job, and it always will be.

Write & Discuss: Bare Minimum Requirements

What are your nonnegotiable or bare minimum requirements for physical and mental health? What are the daily and weekly activities that make you feel strong, happy, and healthy? In other words, what are the minimum standards you need to hit in order to feel great?

Think about it. Have a discussion with a friend and brainstorm ideas. Write them down.

My bare minimum requirements:

Beauty

_____

_____

_____

_____

_____

Nutrition

_____

_____

_____

_____

_____

Nature

_____

_____

_____

_____

_____

Fitness

_____

_____

_____

_____

_____

Sleep

_____

_____

_____

_____

_____

Connection

_____

_____

_____

_____

_____

Creativity/Self-Expression

_____

_____

_____

_____

_____

Feel free to add any other categories that you want!

_____

_____

_____

_____

_____

Once you figure out your bare minimums, promise yourself that you'll meet those minimum requirements for the next month. See how you feel. You may be amazed by what a difference it makes. If, after the first week, you're not hitting your minimums, lower them for now until they are attainable. You can always increase them later.

You know when you're on an airplane and the flight attendant tells you to "put on your own oxygen mask before assisting others"? Handling your bare minimums is like putting on your oxygen mask. You're fueling yourself and keeping yourself strong and vibrant, which means you'll have even more energy to give to your kids, to your colleagues, and to your professional projects and goals. It's really hard to lead and inspire other people when you're completely exhausted. You've got to fuel yourself first. Then you'll have the strength that you need to write, speak, march, rally, raise your kids, build your business, start a movement, run for office, or whatever you feel called to do.

It's easier to change the world when you've handled your basic needs first.

Fuel Yourself with Good Food—and Stop Obsessing

Here in the United States, millions of people spend an unbelievable amount of time obsessing and worrying about food. This affects women *way* more, but it does affect all people to some degree. We worry if we're eating the right types of food. We punish ourselves for overindulging. We starve ourselves until the next meal. We go on crazy diets, eating systems, and cleanses. We even have reality TV shows where grim-faced nutritionists barge into peoples' houses and dump their Oreos and Lay's potato chips into the garbage can. We're so food-obsessed. It's madness!

It's been reported that a typical woman goes on sixty-one diets by the time she's forty-five years old. Think that's not possible? Consider this: maybe you start a new diet every year on January 1st. Then you do a swimsuit season diet at the beginning of the summer. Then you try the latest trendy juice cleanse in the fall. Two or three diets per year, every year, for decades in a row...it all adds up. It's a massive amount of time and mental energy that we women are funneling into gimmicky diet systems that don't even work, at least not for long.

Here's the thing. I *do* recommend educating yourself about nutrition so that you can feel empowered in your weight and health. It's frustrating when you don't feel and look the way you want, and incredibly disempowering when you've tried a million different things without getting the results you're after. I think working with a qualified nutrition professional can create a foundation of healthy sustainable habits that can support you for life. Notice that I said "sustainable habits," not "dieting."

I read a powerful quote online that perfectly sums up the problem with most diets, which tend to have us adopting habits over the short term that we wouldn't want to sustain over the long haul. It said:

> *"The problem with focusing on the outcome is that an outcome has a fixed time of arrival and an impending sense of relief and fulfillment. Then what? That sense of completion = relapse."*
>
> —Excerpted from skillbasedfitness.com

There's a life coach and feminist activist named Susan Hyatt who helps her clients stop the crazy cycle of dieting and regaining the lost weight. She once wrote, "Dieting is robbing you of your life." It's sad to think that every minute you spend obsessing about food is a minute that you'll never get back. You could be using all of those minutes to read bedtime stories to your kids, explore your city, hang out with friends, take an interesting class, or make a difference in your community. There are so many amazing things you can do with your time. Obsessing about food is just so...boring.

I'm not immune to food drama. Before a fitness photo shoot, I used to spend three days drinking nothing but juice—a sad little crash diet that gave me hardly any of the macronutrients and energy my body needed; though it then left my stomach looking flat for a few days, I made that effort only to gain everything back within a week. It was pointless and, when you think about it, the resulting photos were false advertising! They didn't represent the results my actual lifestyle produced. Over time, I've come to realize that deciding what to eat doesn't have to be a dramatic, agonizing experience. It can be simple and enjoyable. Here are some of the practices that work for me and my family:

Nutrition 101

If you're lost about what to eat, I feel your pain. There are so many conflicting articles and books each claiming to know the "perfect" or "right" way to eat. I try not to listen to the latest "news" in nutrition because the headlines are always changing, and there's always some new hyped-up trend. Instead, I stick to these basic principles, which I've learned from working with a credentialed nutritionist:

Make a List of Automatic Meals

As you've probably gleaned from the earlier chapters in this book, I hate wasting time! I'm all about efficiency. I like having go-to outfits that I can throw together quickly—like a daily uniform. I've got my favorite workout classes that I attend every week. In terms of my health and appearance, I have bare minimum standards that I can hit every day without really thinking about it. I try to create that same type of efficiency when it comes to food, too.

I've got a repertoire of about ten to twelve healthy, tasty meals that I love and that I can make really quickly: three or four breakfast options, three or four lunch options, and three or four dinner options. When it's time for a meal, I don't agonize over what I'm going to have. I just think about my catalog of options, and then I choose whatever strikes my fancy. I pick something and I eat it. It's automatic; no drama—the end.

For breakfast, I'll usually make a big smoothie with fruit, greens, water, and protein powder, sometimes with a little Greek yogurt for extra protein. Or I'll make a breakfast sandwich with mashed avocado, spinach, and two eggs on some high-quality bread. I love Ezekiel bread because it's got minimally processed ingredients and sprouted grains, which are so good for you. Or I'll make a breakfast burrito with eggs, salsa, and a little cheese wrapped in a tortilla. Soft corn tortillas are my favorite; they're so good if you put them in the toaster oven first. All of those breakfasts take me about ten minutes to prepare. I keep the ingredients that I need on hand at all times, so it's super easy.

If I'm out for lunch, I'll grab a big salad with some type of protein like chicken, shrimp, salmon or tofu, plus apples, a few nuts, and tons of greens. If I'm seriously pressed for time, I might get a pre-made egg sandwich from Starbucks while I'm grabbing some coffee. They've also got a protein box that may not be gourmet, but which works in a pinch! (I must admit I never pack a lunch, although I know it is probably healthier and more cost-effective.) At home, I often have leftovers from the previous night's dinner.

For dinner, I love making things with my slow cooker or pressure cooker. For example, I can toss some meat or veggies and seasonings in there, turn it on, and walk away and forget about it; and later, I've got a base for the night's meal and plenty of leftovers to use in other recipes throughout the week! It's the laziest way to cook, which is perfect for me because I don't enjoy long, labor-intensive cooking projects AT ALL. I like making a big pot of simmered chicken about once a week, and then I'll use that meat in all kinds of different ways—maybe as a filling for tacos with avocado, cabbage and lime juice, or perhaps in some tortilla soup, whatever sounds good that day.

At this point, eating well has become an automatic habit. It's just like checking my email or grabbing my favorite type of shampoo off the shelf at the store. I don't really think about it, I just do it. Some weeks things roll more smoothly than others, but overall, it's a pretty automatic process.

I recommend browsing through some beautiful cookbooks and blogs to get some healthy cooking inspiration. Then make a list of ten to twelve meals that look tasty and nutritious and seem simple enough to whip together. Get the ingredients you need at the beginning of each week. You can even use the same meals and shopping list for a whole month or season before switching it up. It can be that simple.

Don't Overthink It

Don't you feel bewildered sometimes when it comes to food? You wander through the grocery store picking up different packages and wondering, "Is this healthy? Is this unhealthy? The label says it's 'all natural'—that means it's good for me, right? But wait, what about all those carbs? Are carbs good or bad? Ugh. What the hell am I supposed to have for lunch? Why is this so complicated?" And then you rip off your shirt like the Hulk and run up and down the aisles asking strangers, "WHAT CAN I EAT?" (OK, maybe it's not quite that dramatic, but almost!)

Look, you can read blog posts, magazine articles, and books on nutrition from now until the end of your life, and every single piece of literature will urge you to do something slightly different. My advice? Rely on a few simple rules to determine if something is healthy and nutritious or not: fill a quarter of your plate with your main protein for that meal, half of your plate with veggies, and the last quarter with fats and/or carbs. Try to eat minimally processed foods. Notice how you feel after eating things, and learn what makes you feel best.

To Avoid Feeling Hungry and Cranky, Base Your Meals Around Protein

Everyone's body is different, and some of us need more protein than others. If you feel totally in the dark about your nutritional needs, I do recommend seeing a professional nutritionist. Even just one session can be very illuminating as long as you communicate with them what your goals are.

Personally, I feel best when I base every meal around some type of protein. I always try to make protein the center of my meal, then fruits and veggies, and then healthy fats and carbs. If I skimp on protein, I usually wind up feeling hungry and cranky, or I have a big energy slump in the mid-afternoon. I don't have much experience with vegetarian or vegan eating, so my suggestions might not be as helpful if you are a more plant-based eater. However, some great sources of non-animal protein are tofu, tempeh, edamame, peas, beans, and vegan protein powder, to name a few.

Keep It Fast and Simple

I like simple recipes with minimal ingredients. I'm not the Martha Stewart type. I don't care about baking my own bread or making sauces from scratch, and you're not going to find me basting a chicken on a Sunday afternoon. If you're into that sort of thing, that's amazing, and please invite me over for dinner sometime, because I bet mealtime at your place is incredible. But personally, I'd rather be doing almost anything else!

I typically pick up premade sauces from the grocery store—curry sauce, tomato sauce, pesto, things like that—and then I grab some meat, fish, eggs, cheese, Greek yogurt, pre-cut or bagged veggies, fruit, rice, tortillas, and some nice bread. That's pretty much all I need to whip together most meals. Also, I love getting groceries delivered straight to my house. It usually only costs ten dollars or less per delivery, and it saves so much time. Totally worth it!

Treat Yourself...to Moderation

I try to maintain an 80–20 balance when it comes to food. I make sure I'm eating healthy, nutritious food that makes me feel strong and energized (protein; whole grains like oats, rice, and quinoa; fruits, veggies, and nuts, etc.) 80 percent of the time. I might be a little more decadent and enjoy indulgent food that's purely just for fun—like a glass of champagne or a brownie—20 percent of the time.

I'm not crazy strict about this. Most days, I hit that 80–20 balance without exerting too much effort. It happens automatically. Around the holidays, it's more like 60–40, and when I'm on vacation, sometimes it's been more like 50–50. Once in a while, that's fine. Sometimes you want to indulge in a fancy, decadent brunch with buttermilk waffles, biscuits and gravy, and a round of mimosas, and that's great! But after that kind of meal, you're probably going to feel sluggish and ready for a nap. You'll feel tired rather than powered up and ready to conquer the day. So, it's not the type of meal you want to have every single day. It's a special occasion meal, not your daily fuel. I know that I feel and look my best when I hit that 80–20 balance, so most days, that's where I try to land.

I totally believe in treating yourself to all of your favorite foods. Just keep things in moderation. Also, if you're going to have a treat, make it something that's worth the indulgence. Don't eat a stale, crappy, processed cookie that's not even tasty. If you're going to eat a cookie, get a warm, freshly baked cookie that's mind-blowingly delicious. There's a place called Insomnia Cookies here in Boston that I love. Their S'Mores cookie is insanely good. It's fun to splurge occasionally, I just try not to do it every single day. Again, it's all about moderation.

One more note about "treats." I encourage you to tune in and notice for yourself what truly feels like a "treat" and what doesn't.

Sometimes we perceive things as a "well-deserved splurge" that in reality, are more like a "cruel punishment" to your body—I'm looking at you, third round of margaritas! If the treat makes you feel like garbage, ditch it and find a better one! If you'd like help limiting your intake of alcohol, I highly recommend *The Easy Way to Control Alcohol* by Allen Carr. He also has several other books designed to help you control other habits you might like to quit, like smoking and sugar.

Be Realistic about What You're Willing to Do

I used to get a box of organic veggies delivered to my house every week. It was one of those CSA (community supported agriculture) programs where you pay thirty or forty dollars and then you get a big, bountiful box of fresh produce from a local organic farm. The produce arrived right from the soil, straight to your doorstep. It seemed like a great idea, at least in theory. In reality, I never used many of the veggies. I'd stare at those big unwashed heads of lettuce and bunches of carrots covered with flecks of dirt, and I'd think, "Ugh. Just no." I didn't feel like washing, peeling, and chopping all of those vegetables. Neither did anyone else in my household. Tragically, the produce would rot inside the fridge, and then I'd have to throw it away, which made me feel guilty.

Eventually I realized, "Hmm, obviously this isn't working. I should just get pre-cut veggies from the grocery store, because that's what I'm realistically going to eat." I canceled my veggie-box membership, and that was that. The bottom line is that I'm far more likely to eat vegetables if I don't have to wash and cut them myself. Some might call that lazy. But whatever you call it, that's the reality of my life. I've learned this about myself, and these days, I plan accordingly.

I know people who get meal ingredients delivered by companies like Blue Apron, and they love it. I know other people who grab a big pre-made salad on their way home from work; and still other people are obsessed with their Instant Pots and love simple, five-ingredient recipes that take almost no effort.

I often say to my clients, "The right type of exercise is...whatever you're actually willing to do." It's the exact same thing with food. The right type of healthy food is...the healthiest thing you're willing to make and eat.

You might be fine with throwing together a quick stir-fry, but maybe roasting vegetables in the oven sounds completely tedious. Or maybe you don't care about making your own turkey meatballs from scratch, because the ones from the local deli counter are just fine. Cool! Be realistic about what you'll actually do, and then do it.

Set It and Forget It: Your Fave Meal Ideas

Write down ten to twelve meal ideas that feel simple, realistic, healthy, and almost automatic—meaning, you could easily throw these meals together without any drama. Post these meal ideas on your fridge—or save them on your phone—to prevent yourself from slipping into a state of *"What should I eat today?"* mind-spinning confusion. Just refer back to your list, pick something that sounds good today, and you're all set! You will save yourself so much time.

Breakfast

1._____
2._____
3._____
4._____

Lunch

1._____
2._____
3._____
4._____

Dinner

1. _____
2. _____
3. _____
4. _____

Sneaky Things That Are (Probably) Impacting Your Health

If you've ever played a video game like Super Mario or Mortal Kombat, you can picture that "energy bar" that represents your character. A full bar that is all green = full power. A half empty bar = uh-oh, you need to refuel ASAP. An empty bar that's red and flashing = you're dead—game over.

All throughout your day, you make choices that either keep your bar full or drain it. And sometimes, we engage in certain habits that sap away our health, and were not even aware of how much these habits are impacting us. They can be sneaky little habits, things you barely even notice you're doing, like...

Keeping Electronics in Your Bedroom

Sleep specialists unanimously agree that keeping electronic devices in your bedroom is a bad idea. Electronic light—whether it's from a TV, iPad, smartphone, or digital clock—disrupts your natural sleep patterns. You struggle to fall asleep, and then you feel tired even when you get seven, eight, or nine hours of sleep. Get them out of your bedroom. Switch to an old-school alarm clock that doesn't emit any light. Read an actual book in bed instead of your Kindle. Banning electronics from your bedroom is a smaller change than you might think, but the impact on your health can be huge.

Obsessively Checking Social Media

The average person will spend five years of their life on social media, according to a recent study. Five years! That's a lot of time. Imagine reclaiming all of that time, and imagine what a positive impact it would have on your health, your career—all of your goals. In five years, you could get a master's degree, you could backpack across every continent, you could raise enough money to buy shoes, pencils, and books or even build an entire school for thousands of disadvantaged kids in Cambodia. I'm just sayin'. There's a lot you could do with that time.

Don't let social media own you. Install a plug-in for your internet browser so that you can temporarily block certain sites, like Facebook or Instagram. I love "News Feed Eradicator" for Facebook, which allows you to just check your notifications without ever getting sucked into the news feed.

If expressing yourself or sharing your work online is important to you, preschedule your posts once every month or two using services like Planoly and Meet Edgar. Then check in on responses for just a few minutes a day via computer and delete the apps on your phone. Alternatively, you can limit social media use on your phone by utilizing iPhone's Screen Time feature, or download an app like "Moment," which will tell you how much time you've spent on your mobile device. I also love the "Forest" app, which allows you to set a timer and then yells at you for picking up your phone before the timer is done.

Try curbing your social media time. See how it feels. I promise: you won't miss anything important. And what you'll gain—mental headspace, more energy, room to breathe—is so much more valuable than anything you'll find on Twitter, Reddit, or the comments section of Buzzfeed.

One more thing: remember in Chapter 1 when I mentioned that social media can be a great place to explore your feelings of envy? I would like to add a caveat. There is no rule that says you have to continue following social media accounts that consistently trigger crappy feelings, like your ex's new girlfriend, or a fitness "professional" who uses body shaming to "motivate" followers, or a fashion blogger who performs a lifestyle of sunsets, fancy dresses, and yacht parties, sending you into a comparison funk. I'm not saying these people are "bad," "toxic," or anything that dramatic. Still, you can own your reaction to them and decide you'd be better off with less of this in your life. After all, isn't the whole point of social media to be able to customize who and what you'd like to follow?

Sitting Way Too Much

It's been said that "sitting is the new smoking." Sadly, it seems this is true. If you're sitting at a desk for four to eight hours a day, you are literally shortening your lifespan. Even if you exercise daily, that's not enough to counteract the negative effects of all that sitting. It has not only been linked to obesity, increased blood pressure, and muscular issues, but also diabetes, heart disease, and even cancer.

The only solution is to *stop sitting*—literally stand up. Invest in a standing desk. You can find them on Amazon for thirty to three hundred dollars, depending on how much you want to spend. I got mine at IKEA for under three hundred dollars. Or Google "DIY standing desk," and you'll see how to create one using piles of books. It might take some adjustment as you get used to typing and working standing up, but after a few days, it will feel totally normal—and your body will feel so much better. You can get an adjustable stool to go with your new desk so that you can alternate between sitting and standing throughout the day.

Whether it's removing electronic lights from your bedroom, detoxing from Facebook, or standing more and sitting less, there are so many ways to upgrade your health. Some upgrades are quick, easy, and free with instantaneous benefits. Others require more grit and a longer time commitment. It's all worth the effort.

Anything you can do to reclaim your body and improve your health, I'm urging you: *just do it*. Investing in your heath is a no-risk investment, because it *always* pays off.

Perfection Is Not the Goal

When it comes to your physical and mental health, perfection is not the goal. Having shredded abs and Olympian strength is not necessary for most of us. *Feeling good* is the goal. If you feel strong and confident, if you feel satisfied with how you look, and if you've got enough energy to tackle your day, in my opinion, that's the definition of good health.

So, keep it simple. Set reasonable goals. Hit your minimum baseline of self-care each day, or as often as you possibly can. If you do that, you'll feel great, and you won't feel so preoccupied with your body. Instead, you'll be able to focus your attention on bigger things, like volunteering for a cause you care about, finishing your thesis paper, opening your own Etsy shop, or whatever you want to do with your one precious and beautiful life.

Take excellent care of yourself, because the world needs all the love, talent, and energy that you can possibly provide.

Susan Hyatt | SHyatt.com

She Owns It: Susan Hyatt

Allow me to introduce you to my friend Susan Hyatt, Master Certified Life and Business Coach and author of *BARE: A 7-Week Program to Transform Your Body, Get More Energy, Feel Amazing, and Become the Bravest, Most Unstoppable Version of You.* Her number one passion is helping women get more of whatever they crave. Her philosophy is: if you crave it, then you can create it.

ANDREA. You weren't always as happy and comfortable in your body as you are today. At what point in your life did you realize, "I have to take ownership of my health"? What was the wake-up moment for you?

SUSAN. I struggled with food and body image starting at age eleven. I was confident as a young girl until someone told me that my "thighs were getting fat." So, began my struggle with trying to conform to societal standards and be as thin as possible. By age thirty-four, I had tried just about every diet available and had spent twenty-three years yo-yo dieting.

At thirty-four, I found myself sitting in my kitchen eating an entire wheel of Brie and washing it down with wine while my kids were doing homework at the dining table. I looked over at them, exhausted and numb, and realized that I wanted them to see a different mom: a mom full of life, energy, and passion. I hired a coach the next day.

ANDREA. What kinds of things do you do every day—or every week—to take care of yourself?

SUSAN. I believe that self-care is my best business plan. I'm devoted to being a woman who takes exceptional care of herself. For me, that means seven or more hours of sleep every night, a five-mile run five days a week, and weight lifting three mornings a week. Self-care means asking myself, "Does this feel like love?" Whether it's food, movement, or an activity, that is my litmus test.

ANDREA. Is it hard to take good care of yourself? Is it a constant struggle for you? Or have things become pretty routine at this point—like, you don't have to really think about it, you just do it?

SUSAN. For me now, eleven years later, it's as natural as breathing. I have a routine that works for me, and I do it because I love how I feel when I do. If someone is just starting out, I remind them that self-care is like flexing a muscle...the more you do it, the easier it is and the stronger you get!

ANDREA. What are some of the most important tools or practices in your BARE Program that create the most amazing shifts for your clients and readers?

SUSAN. Dropping the "transactional" relationship with the body. No longer is it, "I'll eat this or do this workout if my body shrinks and tones." It's more like, "My body needs great food and movement to power up." Answering the question, "What feels most like love?" is one of the most transformational things you can do. Also, community is everything. Don't go it alone; being a part of the BARE Daily online community where there is support from other people working through the BARE Program and BARE Coaches to help.

ANDREA. What about mental health? How do you keep your mindset in a positive place? Do you have a gratitude practice? Do you journal, meditate, or take long walks on the beach? Do you see a therapist or life coach?

Susan. Just like I encourage my clients to surround themselves with people who "have their back," I do the same. I'm a part of a supportive Mastermind group that I love.

Part of the BARE Process is something I call Environmental Detox, which is so important for our mindset. Not just what's in your living room, but the messages that we surround ourselves with, too. As a part of this process, I make sure to curate my environment, social media included. If it's negative, it's not getting in. And, of course, thought work is key. Reframing negative self-talk to thoughts that serve is a major part of mental health care.

Andrea. Taking good care of yourself requires some advance planning—like keeping healthy groceries in the fridge or scheduling workouts in advance. How do you stay organized? What are some of your tips and systems?

Susan. I love my Instant Pot! I've never been big on cooking, but I can make a simple, fulfilling homemade dinner in like fifteen minutes. My workouts are on my calendar and are just as important as the rest of the appointments on my calendar—that's nonnegotiable. Also, I do things that I love doing. It doesn't take a lot to get me on a hike with my best friend on the weekend, because I love doing it! Same with the gym and my morning runs. I have a plan that gives me PLEASURE. So, of course I'm going to do it.

Andrea. If every woman on earth took ownership of her health and started taking excellent care of herself, how do you think that would impact our world?

Susan. When we take excellent care of ourselves, we are so much more present and able to do all of the good we have in us to do. If every woman on earth got a "front burner," everyone else on earth would benefit. In addition, think of what a woman could do with all of the time she spends obsessing about her body. I am on a mission to help girls and women break the diet cycle and reclaim that time to change the world.

Own Your Health: Review

1. Do you like how you look and feel right now? If not, what would you like to change?

_____

_____

_____

_____

_____

2. Do you have a tendency to set unrealistic or perfectionistic goals? For example: "I will eat Paleo every single day—no dairy, no refined sugar, no gluten—and I'll do Crossfit five times a week, and I'll turn off my phone every night at five, and I won't ever watch TV unless it's an educational nature documentary."

_____

_____

_____

_____

_____

_____

_____

3. How would it feel to set different types of health goals—like "bare minimum" goals instead of "super overachiever" goals?

_____

_____

_____

_____

_____

4. Do you have a tendency to let other people make health-related decisions for you? For example: does your partner decide when you go to bed? Do your kids' preferences drive what's for dinner? What's one area where you could take ownership of your health and take back some control?

_____

_____

_____

_____

_____

The Keys to Owning Your Health

+ Your body is the only place you have to live, and only you can take care of it.

+ Identify your excuses and give them up.

+ Set your bare minimums and stick to them.

+ Figure out your favorite healthy meals and habits, then set it and forget it.

CHAPTER 4

Own Your Style

Inside This Chapter

+ How to define your personal style and come up with easy, go-to "uniforms" that always make you feel great.

+ Why all of your clothes, shoes, and accessories should make you feel like you're flying first class, not coach.

+ My favorite beauty shortcuts—quick habits that help me look and feel amazing while saving tons of time.

+ Why caring about your appearance isn't "vain" or "frivolous"— and definitely doesn't make you a "bad feminist."

How I Ran Away and Joined the Circus...and Rediscovered My Self-Expression

So, there I was, strumming a ukulele under the stage lights. I was dressed in fishnet tights, a vintage sequined burlesque costume complete with a tutu, and a black sequined top hat. I flirted with the audience from behind a pound of red lipstick and a big, devilish...fake beard.

It was a moment of pure, giddy self-expression. I was putting myself out there: making music, entertaining the crowd, and exploring the boundaries of what gender, beauty, and sexuality meant to me. That fake beard? It was all about challenging the audience to question what "masculinity" and "femininity" really mean. I like to think it was pretty provocative, and at the very least, amusing.

So how on earth did I find myself in that spotlight with a ukulele in my hands?

I was in my late twenties, and I was finishing up my college degree in mind-body wellness and women's studies. After having studied a lot about body image, sexuality, and gender politics, I was inspired to write my final thesis on the "neo-burlesque movement," an edgy type of performance loosely based around striptease which seemed to have powerful potential as a feminist art form.

The "new burlesque" was a medium in which women could explore and express their ideas on sexuality, beauty, and gender, often in unconventional or subversive ways. Having previously worked in strip clubs to make ends meet—a job that had felt mostly transactional although somewhat creative in nature, I was curious about this new art form and its potential to empower women. As I sought out people and experiences to further my study, I serendipitously met two women who have since turned out to be some of the most important people in my life—Carrie Tyler and Crissy Trayner. They were cofounders of the Iron Heart Circus and the same women I mentioned previously, with whom I did my aerial yoga training.

Iron Heart Circus was a troupe whose shows included burlesque, modern dance, acrobatics, clowning, aerial arts, and even a live band complete with a horn section, a theramin, which is an eerie-sounding musical instrument that's controlled by moving one's hands around it to manipulate signals from its antennas, and a curly-mustachioed front man.

Carrie and Crissy were hosting a burlesque workshop that I thought I'd check out as part of my thesis research. I was nervous and excited to see firsthand what this burlesque thing was all about. At the workshop, I was immediately fascinated by an incredible fire dancer named Kiki. But she wasn't the only person who caught my attention. All of the people there seemed so bold, brazen, and confident. Some had long, lean bodies. Some had curves. Some had tattoos. Some had wild, colorful hair. Some had scars on their stomachs from C-sections. Some had stretch marks. Some were my age, and some were older. It was such a diverse assemblage of people. There weren't any snooty attitudes. Nobody was competing with anybody else to be the best dancer or to have the best body. Everyone was there to have fun!

I was mesmerized. I got lost in the music and wound up having an amazingly good time. At this point in my life, I was newly single, and I'd been living in a very repressed, inauthentic way for a long time. It felt so good to let go of my inhibitions and just...dance.

After that workshop, Crissy came up to me and said, "So, are you going to join our troupe? We'd love to have you. We've got a performance coming up soon, and we could use another dancer."

"Um, me?!" I was very surprised by her question. I'm not a professionally trained dancer. Yes, I had done a stint as a stripper back when I was a very young, broke single mom. But aside from dancing around a pole in exchange for one-dollar tips, I didn't have any "performing arts experience." I didn't think I was qualified to join a professional circus troupe. Honestly, the whole idea sounded terrifying. I'd make a fool of myself, obviously! And yet...I was intrigued. Crissy believed in me. She saw something in me that I didn't see in myself, and her positivity was infectious. I told her, "OK! I'll try it out."

The troupe welcomed me with open arms. Before I knew it, I was immersed in this colorful circus community. Over the next few months, I met musicians, costume designers, dancers, acrobats, and cabaret performers. Carrie and Crissy wanted to do edgy performances that really challenged their audiences—they wanted to play with gender roles, make political statements, shake people awake, and provoke conversations. And they definitely succeeded! With these ladies in charge, audiences never knew what was coming next.

I'll always be grateful for the time I spent with the Iron Heart Circus, not only for the lifelong friendships I formed, but for the way it helped shape me. It was a completely transformational experience for me, an experience that felt like coming back to life.

When I joined the circus, I was reeling from a terrible breakup. I'd been so inauthentic for so many years. I'd been suppressing my emotions and wearing clothes that felt like they belonged on someone else. I'd been putting on a very different type of performance—desperately pretending to be someone I wasn't in order to make my former partner happy and to earn other people's approval. I'd practically forgotten who I actually was, what I actually liked to wear, what I believed, and who I wanted to be.

But then, suddenly, there I was, immersed in a completely new world of circus and burlesque performers—where it's all about wild self-expression and liberation. It's an environment where you can wear overalls, or a pony costume, or strip down naked, and it's all your choice, and it's all OK. You can express yourself however you want. You can be completely and totally *you*. It was exactly what I needed to shake any lingering self-doubt out of my system, strip away all the repressive BS, and find my true self again.

During my time in the circus, I started to get creative with my appearance even when I was offstage. I started wearing my favorite colors again, like black and leopard print. (Those are "colors," right?)

I found rock-and-roll t-shirts featuring my favorite bands. I started to bring a little vintage pin-up style to dressy occasions. I put purple highlights in my hair. I gave myself permission to dress exactly how I wanted, and I stopped worrying about how others would judge me. Little by little, I took ownership of my personal style. This transformation wasn't just about my clothes, of course. It was about unleashing my spirit. I was showing myself and the world, "This is who I really am."

Defining Your Personal Style

So often in life, we fall into ruts. Food ruts. Relationship ruts. And of course, style ruts. Millions of people (and I used to be one of them) dress a certain way because they think they need to fit in, to look like a "good mom" or a "serious professional," or because they don't think they're allowed to invest in new clothes that they actually like until they "lose those last ten pounds." They don't like their clothes. They don't feel excited about getting dressed. But they don't feel like they deserve anything better, or they feel overwhelmed and don't know where to begin. So, they remain stuck in a rut, wearing frumpy "mom clothes" that they don't even like, or suffocating inside a "work-appropriate" blazer that feels like a costume.

The problem is, when you're dressing in a way that feels inauthentic, boring, uncomfortable, or unsexy to you, it impacts your life on so many levels. You don't want to pose for photos. You don't feel confident standing up and speaking in front of a room. You feel like hiding. You feel disappointed in yourself. The ripple effect is huge.

Your clothes aren't just pieces of fabric. Your clothes have a direct impact on your mood and your energy levels. That's why it's so important to define your personal style and to start dressing the way you really want to dress. I know from personal experience— owning your style has a powerful ripple effect on your life.

My personal style is always evolving, of course. But most days, I've got things dialed down to a couple of basic combinations that I wear almost every day. I like having these "uniforms" on rotation because I can throw together a cool outfit quickly, save time, and always know I'm going to look and feel like my best self.

Boss Uniform

If I have meetings to attend, I'll usually wear jeans, a rock T-shirt featuring a band that I love, an edgy blazer, and some leather boots. Obviously, I don't care about looking like a traditional entrepreneur. I want to look and feel like myself. My goal is to get people wondering, "Hmmm... Who is that woman? Is she a music mogul? Is she heading to a gig?" Ha! Fooled ya, suckers.

Workout Uniform

If I'm going straight to a barre or yoga class, or if I'm teaching one later on, I'll wear my yoga pants, a tank top, a big scarf, my favorite leather jacket, and some cool bracelets. I'll often wear my Vans slip-on sneakers because they come in so many fun colors and patterns; and they don't have any laces, so I can kick them off in two seconds and be ready to teach!

Fancy Uniform

For an evening out, I have a couple dresses that I love. I think a dress is always the easiest option because it's just one item. Put it on, zip it up, and you're good to go! I love a fitted, knee-length silhouette because it accentuates curves. (It's important to notice what works well on your body shape!) If I'm feeling extra fancy, I'll put my hair into victory rolls to create a vintage look (a trick I learned on YouTube). Then I do red lipstick, black eyeliner, and put on some heels. I gravitate toward platform heels or wedges because they're way comfier than stilettos.

Write & Discuss:
Your New Uniforms

What types of uniforms would make sense for your lifestyle? What would you love to wear every day if you could? Whose outfits make you feel totally envious? Also, what would you love to *stop* wearing?

Chat about these questions with a friend. Poke around on Pinterest for style inspiration. Or book a stylist for a consultation if that's within your budget.

_____

_____

_____

_____

_____

Your Personal Style Is a Powerful Form of Self-Expression

It's not frivolous to care about your appearance. It's not stupid to think about outfits and accessories. When you love how you look and feel, you're setting yourself up for a more powerful day. You're going to have more energy for everything you need to achieve. You'll be happier, and everyone around you will feel it. There's nothing silly about that.

First Class Clothes Only

There's a woman named Alla who is friends with a friend of mine. Every year, when Alla declutters her closet, she picks up each item of clothing and she asks herself:

"Does this piece of clothing make me feel like I'm flying first class—or coach?"

I love that question. Even if you've never flown first class, you know the difference between stellar and so-so. Everything you put on your body should make you feel fabulous. Even your workout clothes and lounge-around-the-house clothes should still make you feel great. I recently got into the habit of buying myself affordable silky pajamas and robes from sites like asos.com, and it feels so indulgent every time I put them on, even though it doesn't cost much money.

Go through your closet and divide everything into two piles: first class and coach. If something makes you feel confident, beautiful, and authentically *you*, then it belongs in the first class pile. Everything else goes into the coach pile. Burn it, donate it, sell it, give it away. That stuff doesn't belong in your closet, and it definitely doesn't belong on your body. It's just clutter. (If you can't part with it right away, move it out of your dresser or closet and into storage for now so you can try living without it for a while. Chances are, you won't miss it.)

It goes without saying, but I'll say it anyway: Clothes don't have to be expensive in order to give you that first class feeling. Price has nothing to do with it. I've bought four-dollar shirts that were on clearance that I love and wear constantly. I've purchased three-hundred-dollar shoes that I couldn't stand (oops) which made me feel totally awkward and uncomfortable. First class is a feeling—a state of mind—not a brand or a price tag. First class can be your favorite David Bowie T-shirt. (Swoon.)

Everything you put onto your body—every shirt, every coat, every accessory—is a form of communication. It's sending a message to you, and also to the world. What do you want that message to be? Think about what type of image you want to project, and style yourself accordingly.

A Quick PSA about Vanity: Caring about Your Appearance Does Not Make You a "Bad Feminist"

I once had a wise mentor in her seventies who made a promise to herself back when she was in her fifties that she would keep getting sexier every year for the rest of her life. She was known for doing fun and spontaneous things, like making her students get up and dance to old-school rap by Public Enemy. During one of her courses, she gestured toward her stylish black bob and casually announced, "I'll never let my hair go gray, because I'm too vain."

Everyone in the class had a chuckle, and in that moment, her matter-of-fact declaration made me instantly more comfortable about something I had always been afraid to admit about myself. I am truly, deeply vain. Why deny it? I love getting dolled up, and I love feeling fabulous!

There's an irritating double standard in Western culture where we are expected to be effortlessly beautiful, but also expected to not care about our appearance, because that's too "shallow." If a person loves their MAC gel eyeliner, gets their hair highlighted every six weeks, or is enraptured over the latest Jimmy Choo shoe collection—then they must be self-absorbed, insecure, or even a "bad feminist" for caring about their looks.

Um, what? Let's get something straight. I want to explicitly say that caring about your appearance *does not make you a bad feminist*.

It is possible to be a smart, ambitious, hardworking, socially-conscious person who's deeply concerned about human rights *and* interested in fashion, makeup, and other aspects of style and appearance. We can be many things, and we can have many passions and interests.

Consider someone like Beyoncé. She's a fierce, outspoken feminist, as well as one of the highest-earning women of all time. She created a scholarship fund to support "bold, creative, conscious, and confident" young girls who are college-bound. She has recorded dozens of songs about girl power, self-reliance, independence, and loving and believing in yourself. She's heavily involved in all kinds of humanitarian and social justice projects—from hurricane relief to police reform.

She does all of that AND she can rock a Givenchy gown like nobody's business. She takes excellent care of her body. She can express herself through her hair, makeup, wardrobe—in all facets of style and glamour. She cares about her image and the message that she's projecting into the world through her appearance. Does caring about her appearance make Beyoncé any "less of a feminist," or any less of a role model? Does it detract from the incredible good she's doing in the world? Hell no! I would argue that putting time into her appearance actually helps her get more attention and amplify her message. And the same could be true for you, too.

Sure, if you *only* care about your appearance and absolutely nothing else, um, maybe it's time to get your priorities realigned. But if you care about how you look *and* you care about plenty of other things as well—personal and professional goals, your health, your impact in your community, your legacy—then hell yes! That's a multifaceted, well-rounded approach. That's being a person of style and substance.

We can head to the next Women's March in DC with our hand-painted signs, *and* we can march in Doc Martens or sneakers or ballet flats. And the next day we can rock Louboutin heels or whatever the hell else we feel like wearing. Caring about your appearance and caring about the world are not mutually exclusive.

If anyone ever tries to shame you for being interested in clothes, style, or your appearance, kindly remind them, "I know it might be hard to believe, but...I can be interested in work, money, politics, friendships, music, *and* fashion and style, and so much more. We can care about *lots of things*—shocking but true!"

Find Your Beauty Shortcuts

I have friends who love doing tons of fancy beauty rituals: homemade face scrubs, essential oils, eyeliner, bronzer, lip gloss, lotions and potions—the whole nine yards. I love being fancy too! What I don't love is spending a ton of time getting ready each day. I mean, I know I have to wash my face and brush my teeth, and I don't mind spending a couple minutes on mascara and a dab of perfume, but it's not practical for me to spend all morning locked away in my bathroom. Instead, I like to invest in beauty shortcuts that don't take much time but that have a big impact on my appearance.

These are a few of my favorite beauty shortcuts. Remember, I am vain AF, and if I could leave my house looking like Dita von Teese every day and still have time left for everything else I need to do, I would. In other words, if you're a no makeup, no razor kind of person, keep doing *you* and feel free to skip ahead!

A Great Dermatologist

To get radiant skin, I'd rather spend sixty minutes in my dermatologist's office once a month instead of spending fifteen minutes putting on lots of makeup every morning. A dermatologist can recommend the right products, oral or topical medications, and treatments for your skin. Finding prescription medications to finally keep my acne under control was one of the most important things I've ever done for my confidence and my appearance.

Aside from helping to find the right prescription or over-the-counter products, there are certain facial treatments that may be available at the dermatologist's office, such as microneedling, intense pulsed light, or laser facials, that can provide amazing results. I have struggled with acne and the resulting scarring my whole life, so for me, these types of treatments have made a big difference. They can be pricey—as much as four hundred dollars or more per treatment, which isn't cheap—but the effects last a long time. Always talk to a doctor to see if they're right for you and if there is a more affordable alternative.

Lash Extensions

Have you ever met someone who's got the most amazing, dark, fluttery lashes, and you wonder, "Are those real?" but you can't quite tell? They're probably wearing lash extensions.

You can get false lashes individually applied to your natural lashes. They last for about three weeks. When you're wearing lash extensions, you don't have to wear mascara or use a lash curler, because your lashes already look totally amazing the second you wake up. I don't get them all the time, but if I'm inclined to wear less makeup, like on vacation or during the summer, or if I just feel like being extra fancy, I'll splurge.

The more budget-friendly option is of course to just use strip lashes, which you can pick up at any pharmacy! They take a little practice, but once you get the hang of them, you can be glam at a moment's notice.

Laser Hair Removal

Sometimes I wonder to myself, "How much time does the average person spend shaving over the course of their life?" Thirty minutes a week? Thousands of minutes every year? The time really adds up! Personally, I think shaving is one of the most boring activities in the entire world, and once you've done it, it only lasts for about a day, and then you have to start all over again. Not to mention the potential for nicks and razor burn.

Not everyone opts to shave, and that's totally cool! If you're someone who shaves, you may want to look into investing in laser hair removal. It works—pretty much permanently—if you're a candidate. It typically works best on people with lighter skin and darker hair, but don't listen to me, check with a professional. The hair does start to grow back eventually, but it's usually very sparse and can be removed with a touch-up appointment every year or two.

Dry Shampoo

I don't know how I survived before this product was invented! You shake up the can, spray it onto your roots, and then like magic, your hair looks freshly washed instead of greasy and gross. It's not a substitute for actually washing your hair, but a little dry shampoo can help you sneak by for an extra day or two. I keep dry shampoo in all the bathrooms at my Barre & Soul studios so that my clients can spritz their hair and bounce right from their workout back into their day. It's not going to bring your hair back from a session that leaves you drenched in sweat (sorry hot yoga, that's why it will never work between us), but it's pretty amazing stuff! I mean, if you've got a lot of hair, you don't want to be washing or blow-drying it more than once every couple days if you can help it!

Gel Manicure/Pedicure

If you're anything like me, you might have trouble keeping your hands still long enough to let someone beautifully manicure your nails, not to mention fitting the appointment into your calendar. I want to go as long as I can between appointments, so I usually opt for the gel mani. It can last about two weeks, and I'm not kidding when I say a gel pedicure keeps my toenails nearly perfect for about six weeks! Since I spend so much time barefoot in the studio, I enjoy seeing that little pop of color or glitter when I step onto my mat.

I'm always discovering new beauty shortcuts. Anything that I can do to save time, I'm all over it. I encourage you to find your own favorite rituals and shortcuts, too. Whatever you need to do in order to feel your best...go for it!

Great Style Isn't about So-Called "Perfection"

I like investing in my appearance. I like planning cute outfits, getting my nails done, and indulging in the occasional facial. I don't think any of that stuff is frivolous. I consider it to be an important part of my physical and mental self-care and an important part of how

I take care of my body, express myself, and communicate with the world. But when it comes to beauty and style, it's important to be realistic and kind to yourself.

Remember that nobody has it all together all the time. Things ebb and flow. Try not to be so hard on yourself if your body, your closet, or your life doesn't look like a picture-perfect, professionally-styled Instagram photo. Mine doesn't either, at least not without a little Photoshop.

Behind the gorgeous photos we see in advertising, entertainment, and on social media, there are many not-so-pretty moments that we don't see; the outtakes, the zits, the hushed-up beauty treatments and crash diets, and of course the photo filters that go into maintaining a flawless image. To paraphrase Steve Furtick, do not compare your behind-the-scenes shots to someone else's highlight reel. And at least once, go for it—get your hair and makeup done, and treat yourself to a professional photo shoot. You deserve to feel like the star of your own highlight reel!

As for the everyday, try to meet your personal bare minimum requirements that you need to feel good. Go above and beyond your minimum standards when you can. Be kind to yourself when you can't. That's my recipe for a stylish, confident, happy life.

Kimmie Smith | AthleisureMag.com

Photo Credit: Paul Farkas

She Owns It: Kimmie Smith

Allow me to introduce you to my friend Kimmie Smith, a woman with an incredible sense of style. Kimmie is a celebrity fashion stylist and the cofounder and creative and style director of Athleisure Media (*Athleisure Mag* and a multimedia podcast network, *Athleisure Studio*) and cofounder and designer of Romply and On Air Style Expert.

She's a woman who doesn't just slap an outfit together. She puts care and creativity into her appearance and that of the celebrities she styles. Every outfit really makes a statement. She knows exactly what type of message she wants to project into the world. She owns it!

ANDREA. Have you always had an amazing sense of style, or is this something that you've cultivated over time?

KIMMIE. I come from a long line of family members who have been in various areas of the fashion industry. A number of them have been designers, product developers, etc. My mom modeled for years, so

I remember seeing her walk a number of fashion shows, and she also owned her own couture boutique where she designed bridal gowns, evening wear, and resort clothing. I grew up being able to have some items designed for me, so my love for wool, velvet, silks, etc. came from that. My sense of style has always been statement-oriented, as I enjoy rocking a pair of jeans and leggings with fun tops and accessories that use exotic skins, stacked bracelets, and everything with sparkle and visual texture. Whether you're looking at the magazine for my style looks or you see my celebs on the red carpet, athletes, or Miss Ecuador, you will see those elements in it.

ANDREA. What's your go-to uniform for work?

KIMMIE. I live for rompers and maxi dresses in the summer, and year-round, leggings and classic tees and sweaters are my go-to looks. I tend to wear a lot of neutral colors, as I am always surrounded by so much color and I need to have a clean visual space. I also prefer my colors to come through my accessories, and they are best seen when I am in neutral. As an accessory expert, I like showcasing my pieces as well as my hair, which is black and a rich dark blue. In terms of shoes, on-trend sneakers and ankle boots all day every day! I love a sun-kissed look with bronzer that mixes two of my favorite honey shades together with a bit of a hot pink for my cheeks, kohl eyeliner, and a fun nail polish that looks like it's black but is probably a deep blue, green, or rich purple.

ANDREA. What's your go-to uniform for a glam occasion, like a party or going to the theater?

KIMMIE. Where my day-to-day style is more casual and gives me comfort since I never know where my day will take me, my glam style is all about showcasing my hourglass figure. I love mixing monochromatic fabrics together, so whether it is a figure-hugging dress or a throwback to a Doris Day style, which is a fitted bodice and a skirt that flares so that my calves are showcased, I'm in love with that! I love rocking heels that are studded in Swarovski, pony hair, or colored soles. I love minaudiere clutches in exotic skins and of course smoky eyes all day.

ANDREA. What are a few easy ways to make getting dressed more fun and stylish?

KIMMIE. Know your body! What do you want to showcase, and what do you want to avoid? You should always have a section of your closet where there are items that are a no-brainer to wear! Make sure they fit and are comfortable; tailor them if you need to do that—fit is so key. Make sure to find pieces that make you happy in terms of accessories. Are you a shoe girl, a scarf girl, etc.? We all have our thing, and those details make your outfits look fun. If you literally wear the same thing every day, then you definitely want to lean on your accessories more. Find your go-to hair look options—when it is up versus down—and your makeup look. When you're prepared, looks are easier to achieve.

ANDREA. At one point in my life, I was totally dead broke, with two kids at home. At that point, investing in a beautiful, buttery-soft leather jacket, for example, just wasn't feasible. What's your advice on how to start cultivating your personal style and how to upgrade your appearance, even if you're on a very, very limited budget?

KIMMIE. I'm a big believer that you can afford anything if you decide that that is what you want. Someone may be able to buy a thousand-dollar jacket with little thought, and someone else may end up getting the same jacket by squirreling away money and getting it at a sample sale or at a major discount at a department store! I believe that you should have a plan in purchasing. Bottoms get a lot of wear and tear, so spending money on these items are key. Outerwear and jackets are also an area that I would ensure you pay a bit more into as they get a lot of wear. Invest in tailoring and dry cleaning or an at-home option to dry cleaning. With tops, you can go either way.

Get a great statement bag. Build your jewelry. If you are on a very limited budget, [go to] sample sales and sites like Rue La La, connect with friends who work in fashion that can hook you up with a friends and family deal, or consider borrowing pieces from friends and family to get you through.

We live in a time when there are stores and brands who are creating essential collections that are meant to pinpoint basics of style at a competitive price point. There are options like in-house brands at Saks Fifth Avenue where a number of items are under one hundred dollars, also Zara and Forever 21, as well as going to consignment shops. (One major tip: go to the stores in this category that are near where fashionable people live and work; you'll find great pieces well below market). The barrier to style has never been so minimal!

Own Your Style: Review

1. When you get dressed, do you feel like you're expressing yourself in an authentic way? Or does it feel like you're putting on a costume?

_____

_____

_____

_____

_____

2. What do you want your style to say about you? What do you want to tell the world? What do you need to wear to do so? What do you need to *stop* wearing? If you're not sure, get on Pinterest and start poking around to see what inspires you!

_____

_____

_____

_____

3. Your personal style is part of how you communicate with the world. What are some words and phrases that you want to communicate through your style? For example: *Serenity, Integrity, Compassion, Protector, Crusader, Life of the Party, Athlete, Visionary, Wild Creativity, Bombshell,* etc.

_____

_____

_____

_____

_____

4. Is it time to declutter your closet? Could you schedule a date and time—right now—to do that? As you begin to look at your wardrobe, ask yourself, "First class, or coach?" Make it fun! Invite over a few friends. Swap clothes. Make a big pile of things to donate or sell. Turn it into a style party!

_____

_____

_____

_____

_____

5. What are some go-to outfits—like daily uniforms—that would make you feel amazing, and that you could start wearing right away?

_____

_____

_____

_____

The Keys to Owning Your Style

+ Style is self-expression. It is part of your nonverbal communication.

+ Come up with your go-to uniforms and use them.

+ Treat yourself to clothes that feel like "First Class," whatever that means for you!

+ Vanity can be feminist AF.

+ Find your beauty shortcuts and use them.

+ Fuck perfection. No one "has it all together."

CHAPTER 5

Own Your Career

Inside This Chapter

+ How to deal with "imposter syndrome"—the fear that you're just not good enough or smart enough to have the career you really want.

+ How to know when it's time to level up and pursue a new career goal.

+ How I set badass career and business goals, and why it's crucial to tell people about what you're pursuing.

+ How I stopped saying "I don't know how..." and switched to "I can figure it out."

+ The "confidence gap": Why most women underestimate their intelligence and competence, whereas men tend to overestimate theirs.

+ How to release "mom guilt" and pursue whatever kind of career you want, even if you've got kids at home.

+ How to bounce back after a setback—like a negative comment from a customer or a piece of criticism from a colleague.

+ The power of the question, "Why not me?"

Do I Even Deserve to Be Here?

Not so many years ago, I was a struggling single mom—I had no credit, no college degree, no job, and no money. I'd be lying if I said I didn't feel hopeless on a regular basis, especially when comparing my life to what I saw around me.

Each day, after my seven-year-old son caught the bus to school outside of our tiny apartment, I would push my one-year-old daughter's stroller down the sidewalks of a town that seemed picture-perfect, full of people who looked like they came out of a J. Crew catalog on their way to important meetings, coffee dates, and social engagements that filled their comfortable lives.

I walked to a studio where I was trying something new—with excitement, but so, SO much fear. I was training to be a barre teacher. I loved barre classes, I knew that. But I wasn't a "good" teacher trainee. I fumbled over my words and feared the sound of my own voice. I was undoubtedly my own worst critic, at a time when the last thing I needed was self-criticism holding me back.

"Practice getting your words out," my trainer would say. "Count aloud when you're alone in the car to get used to it." But even then, with no one around to hear me, the second I opened my mouth, a voice inside my head would insist: *Just shut up, just shut up, just shut up!*

To say I felt unworthy doesn't even begin to explain it. It felt like every cell in my body was made of unworthiness. Who was I to teach these women anything about fitness or well-being? I hadn't been exercising for that long. I was still working on getting back to my pre-baby body. I was in the throes of a long and wretched divorce. That year, I relied on public assistance to buy groceries and on the Salvation Army for my kids' Christmas gifts.

I saw myself as so unaccomplished. What did I have to teach these wealthy, successful, happy women who seemed to have it all? On top of that, some of my students had incredible physiques. They completed each movement skillfully—with perfect timing and perfect posture; really, they could have been teaching the class themselves!

"What am I even doing here?" I wondered. "Do I even deserve to be here?"

How could I present myself as a "fitness expert" unless I was the absolute best? I needed to be stronger, more flexible, more badass than any of my clients. Otherwise, I wasn't even qualified to teach them. Right?!

Fortunately, no. Over time, I began to see the flaw in this reasoning. Being "the greatest athlete in the world" and being "a great teacher" are not necessarily the same thing. Also, in the fitness industry, clients are drawn to certain teachers or to you as a teacher for a whole host of reasons—it could be your personality, your sense of humor, your message, what you stand for, or even your music preferences. They're not hiring you because you hold the world record for squatting 1,102 pounds or because you're stronger than anyone else in the city. They're hiring you because they like…*you*; because they feel good in your presence, get a great workout, and leave feeling better than before they arrived.

Determined to overcome my fearfulness, I took baby steps forward. I used the word "confidence" in my computer passwords, hoping to invoke blessings. I had to type my password-mantra each time I checked my (tiny) bank balance, an incantation of power even in the face of my nearly empty account. Little by little, hour by hour, month by month, I did begin to find my voice. I collected scraps of conviction in the moments when I could at last do a set of push-ups on straight legs, when I could teach a class to a few friends without losing my nerve, when I won a small victory in family court and started receiving the support I needed.

"Where do you get your confidence?" people sometimes ask me now. "You seem so sure of yourself." When I reflect on this, I recall the countless hard-won increments, gathered over many years. Confidence isn't something you can think your way into. You can't get it from reading a book (not even this one, I'm sorry!) Confidence is gained by DOING—doing what you're afraid to fail at; doing what you're not sure you're 100 percent qualified for just yet.

There were no shortcuts for me—no celestial signs, and no surprise inheritance or lottery ticket came to my rescue as I rebuilt my life from rock bottom. And I certainly didn't start a thriving business with multiple locations all in one day. I simply persevered. I kept on, push-up by push-up, password by password. I did one mildly terrifying thing at a time. I forced myself to keep practicing my teaching. I watched my classes improve, little by little. And one day, when I opened my mouth to speak, it was no longer scary. Soon, it was even fun.

The look of fear and shame in my eyes was replaced by shyness at first, then finally by passion and enthusiasm. Becoming a teacher led to eventually managing a swanky studio, then owning one of my own, then two, then five. By facing my fears and showing up again and again, I continue to grow my confidence.

And yet...even though I'm more confident today than ever before, occasionally, that voice saying, "You don't deserve to be here" still creeps into my head. It's like a goddamn cockroach that just won't die. I've learned to identify this voice and to see it for what it really is. It's not the voice of truth. It's just the voice of the inner bully, trying to frighten you and confuse you with "fake news" so that you'll avoid risk. Like all bullies, this voice is loud and obnoxious and severely misguided.

My friend Carrie Tyler, holistic hospice nurse, death doula, yoga therapist, feminist, and general high priestess, calls her inner bully the "itty bitty shitty committee." The next time you hear this kind of voice inside your head, just tell it, "I don't have to listen to you." Ignore this voice and rise above it.

Picture a career goal—anything you'd love to achieve in your professional life. Don't hold back! Be unreasonable if you want. Now, if you were sitting down for coffee with Michelle Obama to ask for some career guidance, what would she say to you? What would your courageous great-grandma suggest? If the US women's gymnastics team was encircling you, what words of encouragement would they give to you? Whatever those people would say, that's the guidance you should follow, and those are the kinds of voices you should tune into. The voice of your inner champion, not your inner bully.

Should you be here? Yes, you should.

Are you capable of reaching for more? Yes, you are.

Do you have what it takes? Yes, you do.

But what if there's a skill you don't yet possess, or a degree or certification that you need in order to move your career in the direction you want? Well, then go get it.

Is it possible for someone, someday to achieve this thing? Then why not now? And why not you?

Is It Time to Level Up?

When I got offered a job teaching at exhale, it felt like a dream come true, like I was now part of the "cool kid crowd"—the best instructors at the best facilities. Getting hired to teach for exhale represented a huge leap upward. To give you a comparison, it was as if I'd been a part-time professor at a tiny community college—a pretty great gig, and one I'd worked hard to achieve! But now, I was teaching at the Harvard of the fitness world.

As I mentioned earlier in this book, exhale is a fitness company that offers spa services, too, like facials and massages. It's all about health and wellness and helping people to de-stress and recharge. The facilities are gorgeous—everything is creamy white and taupe and very serene and dreamy. Working there, I had amazing colleagues and mentors. Over the course of several years, I was promoted from trainee to teacher, and then from teacher to manager, and eventually I got to mentor and train new teachers myself. I loved the continual challenges, and my ego loved my important-sounding job title, for sure. The financial security was amazing, too, since in the not-so-distant past, I'd been completely broke.

Years earlier, when I was pregnant with my son, I remember driving my busted-up car to pick up my minuscule paycheck from the temp agency I was working for. But then my car ran out of gas, and I had to walk to the gas station, use the few dollars I had to get gas, and then carry it back to my car. I wasn't able to get my check because by then the office had closed, so I went home and ate marshmallow fluff and peanut butter on the ends of a loaf of bread for dinner, because I was out of groceries and would have to wait until Monday to get my check and cash it. This was the definition of living paycheck to paycheck. And that wasn't even a particularly unusual series of events. That was just...a typical Friday.

Needless to say, working at exhale was a significant upgrade from my lifestyle of years past, and I had enough sense to appreciate it. I felt so grateful to be there. That's why it was so surprising when, about a year and a half after getting promoted to a managerial position, I noticed that my excitement was dwindling. I was losing my passion and I didn't know why.

I felt so annoyed with myself. "Why am I such a quitter?" I thought. "Why can't I just be happy here? What is wrong with me?"

I didn't want my colleagues to know that I was feeling unhappy at work, but I voiced my feelings to a small handful of people—including a new friend, Margery Altman, an executive coach. Margie urged me to complete an assessment designed to help present a clearer picture of your Authentic Self and to uncover what you need to live most effectively and happily. I took the assessment, then we had a follow-up discussion, and she said, "You would do really well as an entrepreneur."

At first, I thought, "Huh? What? I've never run a business in my entire life. Besides, I'm not the independently wealthy type who can afford to take risks. Entrepreneur? That doesn't seem right."

Margie shook her head and explained more, saying, "Andrea, you're amazing at starting new projects and building things, and then you like to move along to the next big idea. You build and then move onward and upward. That's just who you are. It's not a flaw. It's a strength."

What she said actually made a lot of sense. Maybe I wasn't a quitter after all. Maybe I just needed to create a career that would allow me to keep building and evolving, never staying still for long.

Around that time, I had an opportunity to study yoga in Haiti and get a new certification for working with survivors of trauma. This was shortly after the devastating earthquake of 2012, and the country was in shambles. I had never seen anything like the conditions some people were living in. I met families whose homes consisted of a tarp held in place by some rocks. Some lacked food, shelter, medical care, and safety, as crime had risen to unprecedented levels since the earthquake.

And yet, the people I met were so warm, kind, and welcoming. Even though many of them had absolutely nothing—not even basic housing or shoes—they seemed happier than some of my wealthy clients back at home.

Travel has immense power to shift your perspective, and I had certainly never been anywhere as eye-opening as this. I began to really question my assumptions about my career in this place where my "impressive" job title meant absolutely nothing to anyone. "Maybe I don't need this position in order to be happy or feel successful," I thought to myself. "Maybe that's not what's important. Maybe it's time for a change." I was hungry for a new project. Something where I could really express myself. That's when I realized that, just as Margie's assessment had indicated, I was an entrepreneur at heart. I was ready to level up.

How can we know when it's time to level up in our careers? It's different for everyone. There can be many different kinds of signals. You might feel a twinge of dissatisfaction with your current work, maybe boredom or resentment. You might feel envious of a colleague who's doing something that you'd love to do. You may take an international trip that opens your heart and reveals a problem that you'd love to solve. Or you might open a magazine one day at the dentist's office, discover an article about Equus Coaching, and suddenly find that you're overcome with a desire to work with horses, too.

When it's time to make a career change, you just *know*. It might be a lightning bolt or a slow, gradual realization. But when the moment arrives, you'll know it.

Write & Discuss: Whose Work Makes You Feel Envious?

Earlier in this book, I explained that envy isn't necessarily a bad thing. It's actually a very illuminating emotion. It can clarify what you want to bring into your life and what types of goals you should pursue next. I encourage you to explore what types of jobs, businesses, or projects make you feel envy.

Do you feel envious of your best friend's super-flexible work schedule?

Do you feel envious of women like Sophia Amoruso because she turned her passion for funky, punky, vintage clothes into a multimillion-dollar empire?

Do you envy the lifestyle of the late poet Mary Oliver because her career involved so much solitude and serenity?

Do you feel envious of your local flower shop owner because she gets to make beautiful things and work with her hands all day long instead of being chained to a desk?

Do you feel envious of someone you know who is making a difference at a nonprofit?

Do you feel a twinge of envy whenever you see a genius invention on *Shark Tank*, and do you find yourself thinking, "I wish that could be me?"

How does envy show up for you? Is it a sinking feeling in your stomach when that one photo pops up in your social media feed?

Talk to a friend about this, and take turns sharing your thoughts. Write down what you discover about yourself.

_____

_____

_____

_____

_____

How I Set Badass Career and Business Goals

How do I set new career goals? Often, I start by examining what's making me feel envy—like you just did. Then I think about the type of contribution I want to make in my city or community. When I've considered both of these questions, I try to find a way to combine those two things together: what I'm yearning for and how I want to be of service.

Here are a few of my current professional aspirations, keeping in mind they could change anytime:

+ I want to own twenty Barre & Soul studio locations in multiple cities around the nation—or the world!

+ I want to expand our clothing line and online teacher training offerings

+ I want to release meaningful, inspiring books (like this one!) and speak at women's conferences and events

+ I want to produce more events, too, Barre & Soul retreats, for one, but also networking and personal development events for women to help them get ahead

When I'm setting new goals…

1. First, I write it down.

I know some people always write down their goals with a pen and paper. Lately I've been doing mine in a Google doc so I can access it wherever I am. Do whatever feels right for you.

2. Then I try to figure out, "What do I need to do to get there?"

Usually, the answer is, "I don't know." So, then I ask, "Well, who does know? Who could help me figure this out? Who could I talk to?" I make a list of people to email or call for guidance.

3. Then I "go public."

I announce my goal to at least one other person—and I ask for their encouragement and help in being accountable.

I strongly believe that we've got to tell other people about our goals. There are practical reasons for this—for example, your best friend can't help you find a new job if she doesn't know that you're searching for one. Duh. You've got to let her know what you want. But there are emotional reasons, too. There's something about declaring your goal out loud that makes it feel serious and real. Once I have announced something, there's pressure to make good on that declaration. When other people hear you and see you, it changes you. That being said, it's important to share your goals with the right people. You don't want to text a Debbie Downer and let her know about your career aspirations. Nope. You want to text someone who's bubbly, upbeat, and positive. Someone who's going to say, "Yaaaassss queeeeeeen!" not "What?! Are you nuts?"

I have one friend whose knee-jerk response is always protectiveness. Some of his most-commonly used phrases are: "Watch out," "Don't do that," and "Are you sure about this?" His cautiousness is actually one of the things I love most about him. He's the one I turn to for guidance when I'm concerned about an ethical matter. But he's NOT the one I turn to when I'm starting a risky new project.

When I'm starting something brand-new, I turn to my optimistic friends—the people who see possibilities everywhere—because that's the kind of support I need in that moment. Sometimes, you need the friend who's going to say, "Yes you can!" Sometimes you need the friend who's going to say, "Great! Now shut up and get to work." And sometimes, you just need someone to remind you that you can trust yourself, that it's OK if you don't know everything right now, and that you can figure things out as you go along; the friend who says, "You were born for this. You've got this."

Write & Discuss: Your Badass Career Goals

Write down five things you'd love to create or achieve. Don't worry about "when" or "how" or which order they ought to go in. Just write down some badass career or business goals that feel exciting to you.

1. _____

2. _____

3. _____

4. _____

5. _____

Choose one of the goals you just wrote down. Ask, "What do I need to do to get there?" Write down three steps you know you'll need to take. Or, if you have absolutely no idea, then ask yourself, "Who does know? Who could help me figure this out? Who could I ask about it?" Make a list of a few people you could text, email, or call.

1. _____

2. _____

3. _____

Announce one of your career goals to at least one other person. Don't procrastinate on this. Do it right now. It's OK if you don't have a crystal-clear plan yet. Just tell someone. Make it public!

You Can Figure It Out

After realizing that I wanted to start my own business, I felt excited about the future, but also incredibly intimidated. My track record with managing money was not good. My previous work history? Lots of random gigs, and a couple jobs I'd really enjoyed, but I'd never run my own business before. I'd been an exotic dancer, which is a form of self-employment in a way—does that count?

When I thought about opening my own studio, my heart would accelerate with excitement, but then my brain would say, "Wait a sec...I don't know how to do that."

"I don't know how" became a broken-record loop in my head—until I met a woman completely by chance who helped me to ditch that excuse. One day, I was killing time in between teaching barre classes and I happened to wander into a cute little clothing shop. The shop owner was named Alex; she greeted me and we started talking about clothes, hair (I had a purple ombré thing going on with mine), and our careers.

"Oh, so you run your own barre studio?" she asked, midway through our conversation.

"Oh, no," I replied. "I just teach barre classes in other people's studios. I don't know how to run a business. I mean, maybe someday. But I don't know about insurance, taxes, accounting, you know, all that stuff."

Alex didn't accept that response. She told me, "Well of course you don't know how to do those things. Nobody knows how to do all of that at first! I didn't! That's why I hired an accountant and a lawyer to help me." She continued, "If you want to have your own studio, you can do it. You can figure it out." She offered to email me a budgeting spreadsheet and added, "I bet if you crunch the numbers, you'll see that you could be earning so much more if you ran your own place."

I was really touched by Alex's belief in me. She didn't even know me. And yet intuitively, she could see potential in me. I accepted her offer. She emailed me the spreadsheet, just as she'd promised. Back at home, as I filled it out with hypothetical rent and utility costs, I kept hearing her words in my mind: "You can figure it out."

I realized, "She's right. I don't know how to run a business yet, but I can figure it out. Other people start businesses all the time. Alex did. Why not me, too?"

Write & Discuss:
Make an "I Don't Know" List

Think about the direction you'd like to take your career. Maybe you want to start your own podcast, but you don't know how. Maybe you want to start a 501(c)(3) nonprofit, but you don't know how. Maybe you want to write a book and get it published—but you don't know how. Maybe you want to negotiate for a higher salary at your current job, but negotiating makes you feel dizzy and queasy and... you don't know how.

What are some things you want to do or need to do—except you don't know how? Make an "I don't know" list.

I don't know...

_____

_____

_____

_____

_____

Perhaps you can guess what's coming next!

Next, figure out where you could look for information, what keywords you could use to Google what you need to know, what types of classes you could take, or who you could ask for guidance. Figure out how you're going to get the knowledge you need.

Never use "I don't know how" as an excuse for not taking action. I did that for so many years—and it was such a silly waste of time! It's time to change "I don't know how" into, "I don't know how, but I can figure it out," or, "I don't know how, AND I'm going to find someone who does!"

Take ownership of your career goals. Find a way to get the information you need. There's always a way. As attorney and career strategist Ellen Fondiler once wrote, *"Every door can be unlocked."*

You Are More Valuable Than You Think

About a year ago, I reconnected with Margie. She's the executive coach who gave me that key assessment many years ago, the first person who told me, "Andrea, you're wired to become an entrepreneur."

I told Margie, "I just wanted you to know...that conversation with you changed my life. You helped me see myself in a completely new light. Seriously, I'm so grateful that our paths crossed when they did. I don't think I'd be a business owner today if it weren't for you."

Margie's response shocked me.

"Oh, Andrea...when I gave you that assessment, you were so convinced that I was wrong, I really doubted whether the session had done any good. I'm so happy our conversation helped you, because honestly, I thought it hadn't been effective at all!"

"What?" I replied. "No way. Your words changed my life."

We can be so critical of ourselves. We sometimes think, "I don't have enough experience," "I'm not feeling sharp today," "I'm too

162 | Own It All

fat," "I'm not wealthy enough," or "I don't have my shit together," and therefore, "I'm not valuable." But that's bullshit. You are more valuable than you think. Even if you don't know it at the time, your words and actions can still change someone's life—just like Alex and Margie changed mine.

And if you happen to be female, you might have an especially skewed perspective. Researchers who study human behavior have found that, on average, women are more likely to underestimate their performance ("I think I got six out of ten answers correct on this test"), whereas men are more likely to overestimate their performance ("I think I got nine out of ten correct"). This is called "the confidence gap," and it's been written about in magazines like *The Atlantic*, as well as in scientific journals.

So, if you're a woman, and if you're worried that you're not good enough, not smart enough, not effective, not competent, or not valuable...it's most likely that in reality, you're severely underestimating yourself.

Releasing the "Mom Guilt"

Stay home full-time; work part-time; work full-time; what's best for the kids?

This is an unwinnable debate. Everyone has a strong opinion about what's best. My personal opinion is that your kids are important, and their happiness is important, but your happiness is just as important, too. As long as you're doing your best to keep them safe, healthy, cared for at home, you are under no obligation to try to make everything perfect for them or to prioritize their happiness at the expense of your own. What's best for your kids is probably... whatever's going to make *you* feel lit up, passionate, alive, and at your best.

What do you want? What's your dream career? What type of contribution do you want to make in the world? Clarify what you want, own it, and pursue it.

Whatever you do, don't sacrifice your career ambitions "for the kids' sake." Your kids don't need to see a sad, resigned, resentful version of their mom. That's not healthy for them. Your kids will sense your resentment and blame themselves for your unhappiness, because that's what kids do. Instead, show your kids a strong, happy version of their mom. That's the greatest gift you can give to them.

I know a woman whose mother was a professional opera singer. This mother often wondered, "Should I quit singing so I can be home with my family for dinner every weeknight, be a part of the carpool, and do other things like that? Is it selfish of me to pursue this kind of career? What about traveling out of town for performances? Should I do less of that?" She loved singing onstage, but she knew she wasn't like "all the other moms." She worried that maybe her kids wished they had a different kind of parent: a PTA mom, a bake sale mom—a normal mom.

But then years later, when the opera singer's daughter was all grown up, she wrote a Mother's Day card that read, "I'm so grateful that you pursued your dream of being a singer. Watching you, I knew that I could become anything I wanted. It's because of you that I became a writer. You taught me that 'work' doesn't have to be drudgery. It can be anything I want it to be. You paved the way for me. Thank you, Mom."

This is what happens when you own your career and pursue the type of work you really want to do. You inspire everyone around you, including your kids. They're watching you, and they're taking cues from you. So, hell yes! If you want to be an opera singer, own it and do it. If you want to open your own business, do it. If you want to run for mayor, do it.

As a parent, if you decide to pursue a demanding full-time career, then yes, that means you're going to have an exceptionally full plate. And yes, it means you might not be available for every single carpool trip or soccer game. But that's completely OK, because you'll be influencing and shaping your kid's life in a different and equally beautiful kind of way.

The bottom line is: you're the central role model in your kid's life. If you want to raise a courageous, passionate, empowered kid, it starts with *you*.

Don't Obsess over One Setback or One Negative Comment

There was a point in my career where I was teaching three fitness classes five days a week—which is a lot—and I was pouring everything I had into those classes. I worked hard to put together unique music playlists. I found motivational quotes that I'd read to my students. I'd prepare little inspirational "sermons" where I'd share some thoughts on strength, resilience, grit, and perseverance. I tried to make every single class feel like a life-changing experience.

After class, students could fill out comment cards if they wanted to. I remember reading one card that said, "Andrea's classes are *so boring*. All she does is talk about herself. I watch the clock all the time, waiting for class to end."

Reading the note broke my heart a bit. I also felt kind of annoyed. Like, "Seriously, lady? You took time out of your busy day for this? Get a new hobby."

For a couple days, I kept thinking about that comment card. The words echoed in my mind. Never mind the hundreds of happy clients that I taught every month, or the smiling, sweaty, joyful women who had hugged me after class and said, "That was great! Thank you!"—my mind fixated on this one piece of negative feedback.

That's how our brains are wired, unfortunately. It's a biological phenomenon known as the "negativity bias." We're hardwired to remember negative, scary, painful experiences very vividly. It's an evolutionary trait leftover from cave-dwelling times, one designed to help us avoid saber-toothed tigers and other types of danger;

it is a survival mechanism that's helpful at some times, but less so at others.

But we can override this hardwiring. We can remind ourselves, "Hey, breathe, and chill. This isn't an avalanche of negative feedback. This is just one isolated person's opinion." When someone says something that is intensely critical and cruel, at least 95 percent of it has to do with something that's going on in their life; only maybe 5 percent is actually about you.

It's tough, but try not to obsess over one setback, one discouraging comment, or one negative review. Don't let it ruin your day, wreck your confidence, or derail your productivity for the rest of the day. Shake it off and stay focused on the people who love and appreciate what you're doing. Focus on keeping your "fans" happy, rather than trying to convince "haters" to change their minds about you. "You can't please everyone, and you can't make everyone like you," as the news anchor Katie Couric once said. Damn straight. The sooner we accept this fact, the sooner we can move forward with our goals.

Why Not You? Why Not Now?

Vera Wang was forty years old when she started seriously considering a career as a wedding gown designer. She was a late bloomer, comparatively speaking, but she owned her dream and made it happen. Why not you?

Julia Child had never even tasted traditional French cuisine until her late thirties, and she didn't publish her first cookbook until age fifty. She reinvented her career later in life, introduced millions of Americans to French cooking, and started a kitchen revolution. Why not you?

Frank McCourt was sixty-six when his first book, *Angela's Ashes*, became a bestseller and moved readers around the world. Up to that point, he'd spent his career as a schoolteacher.

Hillary Clinton made history by running for president at age sixty-eight—the first woman to be nominated by a major US political party. She inspired millions of women and girls to shatter glass ceilings. Even though she didn't become president, she'll be a shero for all of time.

What is your personal version of "running for president?" What's the big, courageous career move you'd love to make? Why hold yourself back?

When it comes to your career, your brain can generate a million and one excuses:

"I'm too old." "I'm too young." "It's unrealistic." "It's already been done." "It's never been done." "I don't know how." "I have plenty of time to do it later." "Maybe next year."

The only difference between people like Vera, Julia, and Hillary—and everyone else who's made it happen—is that somewhere along the line, each of them decided, "Fuck the excuses—I'm doing this. Other people design dresses, write books, and run for office. Why not me?"

Whatever kind of career you want to design for yourself, own it, and go for it. Make the first move today. Text one friend to confess your dream. Make an announcement on Facebook. Email a mentor to ask a question. Take one concrete step forward. Choose to be the type of person who makes progress, not excuses.

One day—maybe a few months from now, or maybe in a few years—someone will meet you for the first time. She'll hear about your interesting career. She'll learn about the contributions you've made. She'll look at you with starry eyes, and because of *you*, she'll think: "Wow. If she could do that, then why not me?"

Katherine Clark | KatherineClark.house.gov

She Owns It: Katherine Clark

Allow me to introduce you to my friend Massachusetts
Congresswoman Katherine Clark. Her career in public service
is driven by her commitment to helping children and families
succeed. She is a vocal advocate for ending wage discrimination,
protecting women's health care, access to affordable, high-quality
child care, paid family leave, safer schools, and other reforms to
address the challenges women and families face.

ANDREA. During the last presidential election, millions of girls and
women saw Hillary Clinton on TV and thought for the first time,
"Maybe that could be me one day." Do you see a lot more women
getting into politics and civil service than ever before?

CONGRESSWOMAN CLARK. Absolutely! The 2016 presidential election
has led to an outpouring of women becoming involved in politics.
Women marched in January 2017 and then turned that energy into
a campaign for elected office. We are seeing more women run for
office, volunteer, and donate to campaigns than in any previous
election year. They want elected officials who understand the

female experience and will put policies forward that speak to our needs, not against them.

Andrea. OK, let's dream BIG. Let's say you're a woman and you want to become a senator one day, or even president. What is the path to that kind of position?

Congresswoman Clark. The good news is there is not one path anymore. Part of what has held women back was they felt they didn't have the "right" résumé or background to serve at the highest levels of government. Now, we are seeing women from all walks of life running for office. From nurses to business owners to veterans, women are incorporating the barriers and challenges they have faced as features of their campaigns, not as a reason not to run.

Andrea. As a woman in a male-dominated profession, have you ever felt "the boys' club" didn't want to let you in? What happened—and how did you deal with it?

Congresswoman Clark. I have seen it all! I have experienced [everything from] blatant sexual harassment to unconscious gender discrimination. We have to call it out when it happens, which is not always easy. My best coping mechanism is to find wonderful allies and partners to work with and to look out for other women along the way.

Andrea. What's your favorite aspect of your career?

Congresswoman Clark. Every day I meet incredible people who inspire me to fight for policies that will improve other people's lives. Being in Washington gives me access to influential decision-makers and allows me to advocate for policies that hopefully will give everyone in America a path to success. I am honored that my neighbors back at home have given me this privilege.

Andrea. What's your least favorite aspect—something you wish you could change?

Congresswoman Clark. Right now, money has an outsized role in politics. Campaign finance laws give corporations and the wealthy a much louder microphone than the average American. This undermines our democracy. I am heartened by the grassroots enthusiasm and resources that have defined the 2018 election cycle, but we need to reverse Citizens United and to prioritize people, not profits, in our government.

ANDREA. What are some of your career goals right now?

CONGRESSWOMAN CLARK. My focus is getting Congress back on track, which means a policy agenda that puts the American people first. We need policies that make it easier for families to access childcare, affordable housing, and higher education. I came to Washington to tackle the economic issues that impede the success of women and families. It's time to institute civility and camaraderie within Congress so we can get back to doing our jobs.

ANDREA. What do you hope your legacy will be?

CONGRESSWOMAN CLARK. I hope people will say Katherine was always a voice for the people in her district, that she leveled the playing field for women, and that she built a future worthy of our children.

Own Your Career: Review

1. What are some of your career goals right now?

_____

_____

_____

_____

_____

_____

2. Who can you contact for support, positivity, and encouragement? Who are your biggest cheerleaders?

_____

_____

_____

_____

_____

3. Do you have a tendency to underestimate your intelligence, competence, or skills? When you're feeling inadequate, what will you do to snap yourself out of that mood?

_____

_____

_____

_____

_____

4. If you allowed yourself to set a huge, crazy, wildly ambitious, glass-ceiling-shattering type of career goal (your personal version of "running for president"), what would it be?

_____

_____

_____

_____

_____

The Keys to Owning Your Career

+ Use any feelings of envy you might feel to show you what you most want deep down.

+ Break down your career goals into manageable steps and share them!

+ When you don't know the steps, list your questions and start asking around until you find out what you need to know.

+ Being a parent shouldn't mean sacrificing career fulfillment! You deserve to be happy too.

+ Start asking, "Why not me? Why not now?"

CHAPTER 6

Own Your Relationships

Inside This Chapter

+ My personal strategies for healthy, functioning relationships.

+ How to deal with a friend or colleague who's doing something that disappoints or upsets you.

+ "The Four Agreements," and how these four sentences have upgraded all of my relationships, including my relationship with myself.

+ Online relationships, email, and social media: How to keep it classy and meaningful, and not let these be big time-sucks or distractions.

Yeah, It's Complicated

I had a very complex relationship with my father. Growing up, we didn't have much money, but my dad had big dreams for me. He convinced me that I was gifted; he held me to an incredibly high standard and pushed me to live up to my full potential. For all of that, I am grateful.

My dad wasn't a perfect man. He struggled with many demons. At times, he was abusive to my brothers, my mother, and me. In his house, you knew to "come when you were called," which meant to drop everything and sprint to wherever he was seated so that you could receive orders from him, or perhaps a lecture for something you had done wrong. His nonstop smoking led to all kinds of health issues, including COPD and eventually cancer. He had so many patterns that I'd rather forget. Cigarettes were just the beginning.

When I was twenty, I temporarily moved back home to live with my parents. I had a one-year-old baby—my son Roman—and things weren't working out for Roman's father and me. We had been scraping by from one paycheck to the next in an apartment we'd been so excited to move into—until we discovered it was infested with cockroaches. On top of that, I would never be able to go to college if I had to keep working full-time, yet making just enough money to survive. This wasn't the life I wanted for myself or my son. I needed a place to crash until I could figure out a more sustainable way forward.

Even though I knew we would have difficulties getting along, shortly after moving back in with my family, things got worse. I realized that my dad had an addiction to internet pornography. He was on his computer constantly. It was totally compulsive and out of control. Nobody in the family, including me, wanted to confront him about it. It was deeply disturbing to live like that. I ended up moving out and going back to working at a strip club so that I could support Roman and myself outside of that environment.

This may seem like a poor career choice, and it certainly wasn't always the best work environment for me, but it actually gave me a tremendous amount of financial independence and security; I even bought my own condo when I was just twenty-two years old. I was able to make the money we needed by working only part-time hours, which allowed me to spend plenty of time at home with my son, chip away at a college degree, and live life on my own terms.

Finally, years later, I found the courage to say something to my father. I told him very truthfully, "When I visit you at home, I see things on your computer that really disturb me. It makes me feel uncomfortable around you."

I wish I could say that things improved after that, but my relationship with my dad was complicated and fraught with tension right until the very end. Still, I had finally found the strength to say what I was really thinking.

Later, in the period leading up to his terminal lung cancer diagnosis, he became forgetful, mean, and socially inappropriate. One friend confessed to me, "I stopped talking to him because he was so rude to the servers when we went out to breakfast, it just became too embarrassing to go out with him." And that was only how he acted in public—at home, it was worse.

As for my mother, she was first hospitalized with mental illness when I was four years old. Throughout my time growing up, she would go through difficult periods off and on. I believe that her mental illness was exacerbated, if not caused by, the deep unhappiness of being married to someone who was himself so unhealthy.

My father was sick, rude, and difficult to love. But also, I cannot deny that he helped shape me into the successful person I've become. He was there for me during some of my darkest moments. After I escaped a violently abusive relationship—with no money, no job, no furniture, literally nothing to call my own—my dad's initial response was far from helpful. In fact, it was harmful, when he told me I couldn't leave because I had nothing to fall back on. And yet, once I left my ex, my father came around and was there for me, ready to help. He took out a second mortgage on their house to help me get set up with an apartment, and he drove down in his pickup truck to help me track down all the furniture I needed on Craigslist.

I'll never forget the image of him pushing a mattress up the stairs to my new apartment, wheezing from COPD the entire time. He helped me get settled into my new place and restart my life. I know that he really cared about me and that he wanted the best possible life for me. Despite all of his flaws, and despite the hurtful things he'd done in the past, he loved me the best way he knew how.

He died the year that I finally graduated college, the same year I turned thirty. The last time we spoke, he was in a hospital bed, heavily medicated and delirious. He lay there with his eyes closed, breathing heavily. "Are you in any pain?" I asked him.

"You're going to the game?" he muttered good-naturedly, "All right, I'll go to the game with you." With those final words, he drifted off to sleep for the last time.

Since his death, I have learned to take responsibility—to own—my relationships with others. Instead of carrying bitter, angry grudges, I chose to forgive—my dad, my abusive ex, everyone.

Instead of blaming other people for my problems, I chose to take 100 percent responsibility for creating a better life.

Instead of repeating old relationship patterns with my new partner—like allowing myself to be mistreated, suppressing my feelings, putting on masks and costumes, and pretending to be someone I wasn't—I chose to be fully myself.

Have I mastered the art of creating relationships? Nope. I still mess up sometimes. But my relationships have improved radically. I've learned a lot, and I'm still learning.

Strategies for Creating Healthy Relationships

These are my personal strategies for creating healthy, functioning relationships—romantic relationships, friendships, relationships with parents and relatives, and professional relationships, too.

1. If You're in Danger, Get Out

Some relationships simply should not be maintained. If your health is being compromised, or if your safety is in danger, then you need to cut ties and walk—or run—away. That's what I did with my ex—the one who landed me in the hospital. After our separation, I moved far away and got a permanent restraining order. Sometimes, the only choice is to sever the connection as quickly and completely as you can.

2. Consider Their Past. Have Some Empathy.

After he passed, I began to make peace with the memory of my dad by putting myself in his shoes. I thought about his past, his terrible childhood, the religion he was taught, and the pain he had endured. Each time I remembered to do this, I'd feel so much empathy for him. Instead of viewing him as a villain, I saw him as just...a person—a flawed human being, just like me, who was trying to do his best with the tools he'd been given. With empathy in my heart, it was easier to let go of my resentment for the difficult relationship we'd had. I could appreciate the great parts about him and let go of the rest.

If you're struggling to cultivate empathy for someone, try imagining this person as a small child. Children aren't born mean, cruel, or violent. Something happens to shape them into that kind of person. Imagine what this child went through—what they endured, what they witnessed at home, and the type of parenting or resources they did or didn't, receive. Try to envision your "worst enemy" as a vulnerable child, and this can make it easier to cultivate compassion for what they've been through.

3. Take Responsibility for Anything You Feel You Could Have Done Better

There is tremendous empowerment in being the first to apologize. Yes, you read that last sentence correctly! In spite of all the articles you may have seen insisting that women stop saying "sorry," I would like you to consider a different point of view. We put so much energy into being right, defending our position, and blaming others. When we blame, we make ourselves the victim. When we are victims, we have no power, because we're at the mercy of how others have mistreated us. When you commit to *not* being a victim, you put yourself back in the driver's seat of your life.

Be the first to say, "I messed up. I will do better." Own up to anything you feel you could've done better. Say, "I didn't understand what you meant, and I should have asked for clarification;" or, "I ignored the warning signs. That's on me;" or, "I was late. Again. I'm sorry." Instead of blaming others, own up to your part. It shocks people when you do this, because it's the opposite of what most people do. They may not know how to react at first, but in my experience, it helps others let their guard down and clears the way for better communication. (Owning your mistakes is so difficult to do, and so crucial. It's a big topic and it's one that we'll discuss in more depth in the next chapter, *Own Your Past*.)

4. Strive to Leave Other People Uplifted by Your Presence

Every relationship is an opportunity to touch someone's life and leave a positive imprint. Even if a relationship is coming to an end, it's usually still possible to end things on a positive note. (Maybe not always, but it is always worth a try.) You can say, "I respect you and I wish you all the best;" or, "Although we don't see eye to eye on this, I want you to know that I appreciate how you've influenced my life."

Even when I have to fire someone or say "no" to someone's request, I still want that person's life to be better in some way for me having been in it, and I seek to make that possible. I want them to look back on our interactions and feel a sense of validation and empowerment, not frustration or miscommunication.

5. Don't Let Things Fester

Don't ignore people's attempts to be heard. Don't ignore problems that are emerging. Handle it. Say it. If there's weird tension between you and a friend, address it. If you're upset, say so. Try to deal with these kinds of things as quickly as possible. The longer you wait, the more awkward it gets.

Once, I literally ducked out of sight when I saw a woman I didn't want to bump into at Whole Foods. As I quickly pushed my cart toward the organic bananas, I thought, "This is ridiculous. I don't want to live my life like a coward." I vowed to myself, "I won't let things fester like that; never again."

6. Most of All: Don't Be Passive. Actively Create the Relationships You Want.

You can take ownership of your relationships. When I say "ownership," I'm not talking about controlling what others do and say. I'm talking about "owning" what *you* do and say. Another word for "ownership" in this case might be "responsibility." This means behaving with integrity, admitting when you've messed up, deciding what kinds of relationships you want, setting limits and personal policies, and taking matters into your own hands rather than waiting around to be acted upon.

You can decide if you're going to see your parents every week—or not.

You can decide if you're going to share a home with your love interest—or not.

You can decide if you're happy with your current circle of friends, or if you want to seek out some new people and expand your circle.

You can decide what you're willing to tolerate and not tolerate. You can set "hard limits" and "never agains." It's all up to you. Instead of taking a backseat and letting relationships "just happen," take ownership of your part in the situation, and take an active role in creating the kinds of relationships you want.

Vulnerability and Honesty (Just Say It Already!)

Remember my friend Carrie Tyler, one of the founders of the Iron Heart Circus? Carrie happens to be one of the most seasoned and talented yoga instructors I know, and she played an important role in getting Barre & Soul's yoga program off the ground. She's a longtime friend and trusted advisor. I love her like a sister. But a few years ago, our relationship hit a minor bump in the road.

My studio was planning a retreat on the island of St. Croix in the Caribbean. It was a big undertaking: renting the venue, arranging accommodations, flying instructors out to the island, and coordinating meals and transportation. We were getting help from a local St. Croix resident named Kiki, the fire dancer I'd met years ago at the burlesque workshop. Even with her help, planning the retreat was a financial risk. I was feeling nervous about selling tickets. Would we be able to fill up the event? Would the whole thing be a hot mess? I really wanted it to be successful.

Then I found out that Carrie was planning a very similar retreat of her own...also in St. Croix. It was scheduled to happen shortly before mine. "Wait a minute," I thought. "What?"

I knew that Carrie was an honorable person and a great friend. I knew she wouldn't do anything to intentionally hurt me or my business. But this whole thing felt very weird. At first, I didn't deal with it. I didn't say anything. She didn't say anything. Tension built between us. But eventually, I couldn't handle it anymore. I knew we needed to have an open, honest conversation. Finally, I said, "Carrie, this feels really awkward, but I need to get something off my chest because I care about you too much not to say it..."

She seemed like she already knew what I wanted to talk about.

"Look, I love you, and you're one of my best friends, and I don't want to let anything get between us," I continued. "But when I found out that you're doing a yoga retreat in St. Croix that's really similar to my retreat, that felt weird. The students at Barre & Soul look up to you, and some have picked your retreat over mine, so it feels like there's a conflict of interest. Most of all, I was confused that you didn't tell me. I just wish you'd given me a heads-up. I felt like I was in the dark about the whole thing. I felt annoyed, and I didn't want to say anything because you're my friend, but..."

Carrie interjected, "Fuck yes! I've been annoyed, too! I love you so much, but I feel like St. Croix was my turf first. I'd been planning my own retreat for so long, Kiki and I have been talking about it for years; and then you decided to do yours, and I was like, wait a minute, that was my plan first!"

We talked for a few more minutes. Immediately, it became clear that both of us had felt "in the dark" about the other person's plans, and both of us felt irritated that we hadn't been given a heads-up in advance. Not only that, but I learned there were other ways I hadn't been showing Carrie my support professionally with regard to her teaching yoga, and that had been weighing on her.

We agreed that we'd never let that happen again. We came up with a new system: Before we schedule retreats, we will compare our schedules and make sure there's no overlaps or conflicts and that they're not scheduled too closely together. We can both do our own events; we'll just keep each other informed about what's happening and when. We can support each other instead of feeling left out. Most importantly, we agreed to have a 100 percent no-BS relationship, to never let things fester, and to always have open communication with each other.

If you feel irritated with someone—a loved one, an employee, a manager, anyone in your life—express how you feel. It's the only way to have a productive, honest conversation about how to get things back on track. Bottling it up solves nothing. It just makes you feel terrible.

The other lesson in this was that people *hate* being left in the dark, so always communicate your intentions in advance. If you're planning a solo vacation by yourself, your partner would probably like to know about it. If you're doing a personal project that might pull you away from your desk, give your boss some extra advance notice. Even if you think, "Oh it doesn't matter, they probably won't even care," give them a shout anyway. People really appreciate being kept in the loop so that they can plan accordingly. This one shift alone will hugely improve your relationships.

The Four Agreements

One of my favorite spiritual teachers is a man named Don Miguel Ruiz, the bestselling author of *The Four Agreements*. It's a book filled with timeless wisdom on how to lead a satisfying, successful life and upgrade all of your relationships, including the one with yourself.

The Four Agreements are as follows:

1. Be impeccable with your word

Speak with integrity. Say only what you mean. Avoid using words to speak against yourself or to gossip about others. Use the power of your word in the direction of truth and love.

2. Don't take anything personally

Nothing others do is because of you. What others say and do is a projection of their own reality, their own dream. When you are immune to the opinions and actions of others, you won't be the victim of needless suffering.

3. Don't make assumptions

Find the courage to ask questions and to express what you really want. Communicate with others as clearly as you can to avoid misunderstandings, sadness, and drama. With just this one agreement, you can completely transform your life.

4. Always do your best

Your best is going to change from moment to moment; it will be different when you are healthy as opposed to sick. Under any circumstance, simply do your best, and you will avoid self-judgment, self-abuse, and regret.[1]

I've found that when something feels out of whack in my life—when I feel discouraged, unhappy, or stressed—it's usually because I've forgotten to uphold one (or several) of the Four Agreements.

One of the hardest agreements for me is *"Don't take anything personally."* I struggle with that one, for sure. In the winter of 2017, I wrote a newsletter for the Barre & Soul mailing list. This was shortly after the presidential election. I was deeply discouraged by Hillary Clinton's loss, and so—along with hundreds of thousands of other women—I traveled to Washington, DC, to participate in the Women's March.

It was a thrilling, empowering day—a day that gave me renewed optimism for the future. In my newsletter, I shared stories and photos from the march, and I encouraged everyone reading to be active, to get involved, to march, and to continue the fight for women's equality and empowerment. This newsletter was more politically charged than previous newsletters about barre classes and cute yoga pants. I was a little nervous about how people would react. Would they like it? Hate it? Feel irritated about it?

The answer was...all of the above. Lots of people emailed back to say "Yes!" "Love this," "I was there, too!" or, "Thank you for taking a stand!" About ten people clicked "Unsubscribe," which wasn't much higher than the usual rate whenever a newsletter goes out. And four people emailed me to voice their annoyance, saying things like, "I signed up for this mailing list because I wanted updates on fitness classes. I'm not interested in your political opinions." (And some things that were less polite than that.)

Even though it was only four people—just four out of more than ten thousand people I'd sent the newsletter to—it still bothered me. Again, this is because our brains have a *negativity bias*—meaning,

---

1 *The Four Agreements* ©1997, Miguel Angel Ruiz, MD. Reprinted by permission of Amber-Allen Publishing, Inc. San Rafael, CA. www.amberallen.com All rights reserved.

we're biologically wired to remember unpleasant, threatening experiences vividly, and to replay those experiences over and over in our minds. Even if you get four negative responses and dozens of positive ones, it's the four negative ones that feel the "loudest" inside your brain. Those are the ones that get seared into your memory. That's what happened for me. I kept thinking about those four negative emails over and over, fretting and worrying, and amplifying everything into a much bigger deal than it actually was. My mind was swirling with thoughts like, "Should I stop writing anything about feminism or politics? Maybe that's not what my customers want to hear? Maybe I should just keep my thoughts separate from my business?"

For about a week, all of these anxious thoughts ran rampant in my mind, until I decided, "OK, that's enough." I thought back over the last couple days, and I realized that I'd failed to uphold one of the Four Agreements: *Don't take anything personally.* I'd been taking the whole thing way too personally, and it was becoming a huge source of stress and a big distraction.

Who knows why those four people felt irritated about my Women's March story? I don't know. But I know it is ultimately not about me, it's about them and their experiences. It's not something I can control, either. I have my opinions. They have theirs. It's not possible for me to create anything—a class, a retreat, a newsletter—that makes 100 percent of the human population say, "Yes! I love this!" That's not how life works.

All I can do is continue to express myself with authenticity. Some people will love it, others won't get it, and a few will tune me out, and *none of it is personal.*

As the actress, model, and burlesque icon Dita von Teese once said:

> *"You can be the ripest, juiciest peach in the world, and there's still going to be somebody who hates peaches."*

If someone doesn't like my peachy flavor, so be it. I can't change that, and if there's something I can't change, then it's not worth any of my time or mental energy.

Write & Discuss:
Upholding the Four Agreements

If you don't own the book already, do yourself a favor and get a copy of Don Miguel Ruiz's *The Four Agreements*. It's a book—and a philosophy—that have upgraded all of my relationships, including my relationship with myself (my self-esteem, the way I talk to myself, the way I keep promises to myself, everything).

Let's look at each agreement again, one by one. As you read through the list, I invite you to ask yourself, "Am I upholding these agreements in my life? Mostly? Not really? Where are my weak spots?" I recommend discussing the following questions with a friend—a friend with whom you can be totally honest, someone who's willing to "go there" and talk about messy, imperfect aspects of life.

If you don't have a friend like this, please, for the love of Pete, find one, and/or hire a life coach or therapist. (We all deserve that kind of totally honest, 100 percent no-BS BFF in our lives.)

#1. Be Impeccable with Your Word

Are you always impeccable with your word? Do you do what you say you're going to do 100 percent of the time? 75 percent of the time? 50 percent of the time? Does it depend on the promise, or the person, or the situation? Be totally honest with yourself. Do you speak negatively about yourself, or gossip about others?

_____

_____

_____

How do you feel about that?

_____

_____

_____

_____

_____

If you became more impeccable with your word, how would that change your life?

_____

_____

_____

_____

_____

How could you become more impeccable with your word right away?

_____

_____

_____

_____

_____

#2. Don't Take Anything Personally

Do you have a tendency to take things personally? If someone snaps at you, if you get a negative-sounding email, if someone cancels a date, or if you don't get the job that you wanted, do you assume it's a personal attack? Do you assume that you've done something horribly wrong, or that there's something flawed about you?

_____

_____

_____

_____

_____

What's something that would help you to take things less personally? Is there something you could say to yourself? Something you could do? Some way you could remind yourself that other people's reactions are not within your control?

_____

_____

_____

_____

_____

#3. Don't Make Assumptions

Can you remember a time when you made an assumption about a situation or about someone's motivations and it turned out to be untrue? What happened?

_____

_____

_____

_____

_____

Can you remember a time when you made an assumption about what someone was going to do, but then they didn't do it, and you felt hurt or annoyed? What happened?

_____

_____

_____

_____

_____

What is one way that you could announce your own plans, intentions, or feelings more directly to prevent misunderstandings?

_____

_____

_____

_____

#4. Always Do Your Best

When it comes to your personal life—your friendships and relationships at home—do you feel you are doing your best? What about when it comes to your health and well-being and how you're taking care of yourself? How about when it comes to your career and your finances? Your appearance and personal style? Your involvement in your community? Write down some areas where you feel you're really doing your best and some areas that could use an upgrade. Maybe there's an area where you've been too hard on yourself and you could give yourself a bit more credit.

_____

_____

_____

_____

_____

Pick one of the areas that you've decided could use an upgrade. How could you start giving your best effort? Or at least crank things up from 50 percent to 75 percent effort?

_____

_____

_____

_____

_____

Online Relationships and Social Media

Most of us have a love-hate relationship with the internet, email, and social media. Yes, it's incredible to reconnect with your long-lost BFF from high school. No, it's not fun to see an avalanche of mean comments appearing beneath something you've posted. Yes, it's fun to put together a Pinterest collection to map out your dream house. But also, it sucks when you're obsessing over someone else's "perfect" life on Instagram and feeling inadequate by comparison. And OMG, can the endless stream of LinkedIn connection requests just chill for a second?!

In terms of building relationships and communicating online, I have a few policies. Here's how I keep things sane:

Be Truthful

Check your facts. Tell the truth. If you're doing a Facebook post, blog post, or newsletter, say what you actually feel and believe. Don't put on a mask, because that's no way to live your life.

And please, double-check your facts before you share a piece of "news" or "data." There's an incredible amount of misinformation floating around out there, and most people will believe just about anything they see online. Share with discernment.

Be Kind. Spread Positivity, Not Poison

The world is already hard enough as it is. We don't need any more negativity or any more poison. There's no need to post a mean-spirited blog comment, participate in gossipy conversations, or rejoice in a celebrity's latest breakup or publicity scandal. It's not cute to be "snarky." It's just mean.

Set Reasonable Limits

The problem with the internet is that it's free, it's available 24/7, and it's endless! Once you dive into a Facebook or Wikipedia rabbit hole, you know how it goes. You blink, and suddenly an hour has elapsed and you barely remember what you were even doing. It's so important to set limits. I will be the first to admit that I still struggle with this, though I'm working on doing better. I try to limit myself to thirty minutes a day of social media time. Often, I'll uninstall apps from my phone to make it easier to honor this policy. The iPhone also now has a feature called Screentime which will block certain apps for you after a time limit has been reached.

What kinds of limits would make sense for you? Maybe you want to remove a few apps from your phone, too. Maybe you want to keep your phone on silent, or turn off all of those social media notifications. You can also install Leechblock onto your internet browser. It's amazing. With Leechblock, you select a website (say, Facebook.com), and then you set a target (say, twenty minutes a day). Once you've scrolled around Facebook for twenty minutes, boom—the site is blocked for the day and you can't log back in until the next day. You're basically forcing yourself to adhere to the limits you've set. It's kind of like having a parent say, "OK, enough! It's bedtime. Lights out!" And sometimes, that's the kind of love we all need!

For my email, I use something called Boomerang, which has so many great time and energy saving features, I can't recommend it highly enough. One of my favorite features is Inbox Pause, which lets you continue to use your Gmail account to draft and send messages while blocking distracting new emails from coming into your inbox until you're ready to see and deal with them.

Aim for Quality over Quantity

You don't need to be active on fourteen different social media platforms, and you don't need to check in every single day. Keep it simple. With connections and friendships, aim for quality over quantity.

Be Discerning about What You Say "Yes" To

We're all flooded with a million invitations—Evites to parties, Meetup invitations, invites to join private Facebook discussion groups, and of course, trillions of email requests for time, advice, help, a referral, an introduction, you name it. It's a lot to handle. Part of building strong relationships—online and offline—is saying "Yes" only when you *really* mean it.

Don't overschedule yourself and then flake out on six events in a row. Don't join groups that you have no interest in participating in. Spreading yourself too thin doesn't strengthen your relationships. It just fills your mind and calendar with clutter and makes you feel shitty for always bailing and letting people down. (Revisit the tips on saying no in chapter 2 of this book if you need a refresher course!)

Be Respectful. Think about How Your Words Impact Others.

Think twice before you post a pissy Yelp or Amazon review. Remember that everything you write online will eventually reach—and directly impact—a human being. Do you really want to rip apart someone's work like that? Do you really want to publicly humiliate and shame someone in your community? What if that person was your daughter or your friend? Maybe there's a better way to voice your disappointment—a private email or phone call, for example. Online, we often forget that actions have consequences, and words have an impact. Choose your words carefully.

Claim Your Power and Use It Wisely

The internet can be frustrating (and distracting) at times, but let's not forget—it's also an incredible tool. For the first time in history, thanks to the internet, you can write a book and self-publish it and get your message out there—no publishing company required. For the first time in history, you can record your own podcast or host a streaming radio show and launch it—no radio station required. You can do a Facebook Live video to share an important message. You can make a donation—instantaneously—to support a cause you support. You can fact-check something that's being said on the news (or in a Presidential debate) in real time.

The internet has given us so much power. We need to use our power wisely. I've learned a lot from feminist marketing expert Kelly Diels about using the internet as a tool to shape the world. Through her blog, she shares insights on feminism, activism, racism, and many other topics. She doesn't hold back. She writes prolifically and uses the internet to carry her messages far and wide.

Shaun King is a civil rights activist who never stops fighting for equality. He uses social media to share underreported news stories about important political and racial issues, shine a light on injustice, mobilize his followers, and change the world.

Bottom line: the internet can be a distraction, or it can be a tool to further your message, grow your business, touch people's lives, spread inspiration, or lead a revolution. It all depends on how we choose to use it.

Above All, Conduct Yourself in Such a Way That You Feel Proud of Your Communication

With every email, every post, every comment or review, write as though your words are going to be shared publicly. Because who knows? Emails get leaked all the time. Maybe one day yours will be on the front page of WikiLeaks or the Huffington Post. Before you hit "send" or "publish," ask yourself, "Would I feel OK if this was seen by my boss, my mentor, or the entire world?" If not, rewrite it.

It may sound crazy, but if you were to pretend that everything you say (and write) was being recorded by a TV camera crew and might be publicly revealed at some point, it would probably change your behavior and upgrade your relationships. With that imaginary-camera rolling 24/7 and capturing your every decision, you'd think twice before sniping and gossiping with a coworker, snapping at a customer service rep, or flaking out on a friend who's waiting eagerly for you to show up. What if that camera footage was being sent directly to someone you admire? How would you conduct yourself knowing that he or she'd be watching? Would you carry on as usual—or change a few things?

We all have room for improvement when it comes to our communication and relationships. Own up to what's working, what's not, and what you'd like to change. Own it all.

Katherine North | DeclareDominion.com

Nick North | NickNorth.co

Photo Credit: Jen Downer

They Own It: Katherine & Nick North

Allow me to introduce you to my friends Katherine and Nick. They've been married two years, and together they have three businesses, two ex-partners, five kids, amazing friends, and a documentary in the making...all while navigating Nick's transition from female to male. Through it all, they're masters at navigating relationships and communicating clearly and honestly.

ANDREA. There are so many people in your life who need things from you, almost constantly—kids, friends, your clients. How do you attend to everyone without completely burning out? What are your secrets?

KATHERINE. Well, I do burn out. At least once a day. The best trick I know is to go ahead and build a little buffer into each day, week, and month, because I always end up needing it. Instead of pretending that I'll be able to zoom along in perfect balance, I just accept the reality that at some point, I *will* be that hollow-eyed woman staring hopelessly at the school form trying to remember what my own name is. So, I try to build in some room for that woman to recuperate. My best trick is to barter with your spouse so that you each get a pocket of alone time every day (even if it's just twenty minutes when you trade off the kids) to do that recuperating. A quick walk outside, lying down with music on, weeping softly into your pillow—these are all marvelously restorative. (OK, they're not all marvelous, but they can be the difference between flaming out and living to burn another day.) The other thing is to ruthlessly schedule your own real bliss time into the calendar—I'm a fan of a monthly massage subscription, because knowing that you *have* to use or lose it after you've paid for it is a good motivator for busy women. Sometimes the only way to get something in there for yourself is to be ridiculously proactive and schedule things in weeks, months, sometimes even years in advance. (In 2020, you *shall* take that writing sabbatical! The Google calendar says so!) When you get yourself on the calendar first, it's easier to protect that space than to try and squeeze time for yourself in after everyone else's needs are met (which will be never). It's also easier to set a boundary with someone if you have dedicated time for them set aside, as in, "No honey, Mommy can't levitate blocks on FaceTime with you right now, but I will kiss your sweet face at bedtime," or "Sorry, Professor, I've got to run right now but let's talk about this over lunch next month at the conference."

Nick. I am the typical obliger/hero archetype. I hate disappointing people, and I want to have such a full vibrant life that I often will overextend myself, because full and bursting are so very close together on the scale. When this happens I have my feelings, and I ask my wife for help. We communicate a ton about our workloads, and our division of family life labor ebbs and flows based on our workloads at the time. When I'm proactive, this system works awesomely. When I'm not, my body lets me know by making me take sick days. This is a super effective way to convince me to pay attention!

Andrea. When's the last time you had a relationship that felt really sour, strained, or out of whack? What happened, and how did you get things back on track?

Nick. If I'm being honest, five years ago, so many of my relationships would start off amazing, and then somewhere along the way they would go sour. I would end up resentful or having to withdraw completely and straight up ghosting people. Then I went through some big changes: I did so much therapy, got divorced just because I wanted to, fell in love with a woman because I felt love in my heart (and my loins, if we're going there), and accepted the fact that I am actually a man. I got closer to what felt true to me with each and every step toward what I wanted. Once I could say out loud what was true in my heart and soul, it was easier for me to admit what I wanted and what was true in every aspect of my life. The practical everyday practice of that is setting boundaries with the people around you. This is a thing I'm still learning. I think it was only a few months ago that Katherine looked at me and said, "Just because someone texts you, and you see it, and you could respond right now, doesn't mean you have to. Everyone does not have access to you all the time, you know?" And honestly, I don't think I did know. It felt like the first time I had heard it.

Andrea. Nick, it's hard to imagine what it was like to live the first thirty-something years of your life in the wrong body, and in many ways I'm sure it was a huge relief to finally be able to authentically express your true self in the world. That said, it must have been a difficult process for both of you. What was the biggest relationship lesson you learned along the way?

Nick. I think the biggest thing I learned was that I am never willing to allow myself to suffer for the sake of someone else's comfort again. I spent the first thirty years of my life not being happy because I chose my parents' comfort (well, they chose their comfort over mine at first) over mine. I chose what my friends might think of me over what I knew to be true to myself. I chose to be afraid instead of brave. I thought I was keeping myself safe, but instead I was keeping myself small and disconnected. I was limiting all my relationships by limiting myself. I look at the past three years of my life, and I realize that it's been this snowball effect. Every step I took toward living a life that is my own was like a crank up a roller-coaster track, and now I'm on the thrilling ride down the hill barreling toward the double loop de loop. Life is *full* and *beautiful* and *terrifying*, but man, we are living, and we are making it count. To do that you have to stay honest—and a tiny bit uncomfortable.

ANDREA. Imagine you're writing a blog post on "how to become a better communicator." You've got limited space and a strict word count, and you can only share three quick tips. What would those tips be?

KATHERINE. One, don't guess; ask. Two, kind but blunt is always the way to go. Three, every time you find yourself starting a sentence with "I wish..." rephrase it so it goes, "Next time I'm going to try..."

NICK. Our big motto is "Kind and Blunt." It's hard sometimes, it feels terrible to know that something you need to say could hurt the person you love. And yet, not saying it? That causes even more damage.

ANDREA. Fantasy relationship! If you could have brunch or drinks with anyone in the world—and become BFFs—who would it be?

KATHERINE. Michelle Obama. How does she stay so gracious and courageous in the face of it all?

NICK. I'm just gonna stick with it here and say Barack. I can't think of a better example of masculinity in the world right now.

ANDREA. What if there's someone who feels like a huge drain in your life—they're negative, demanding, narcissistic, or whatever— but unfortunately, you can't avoid this person. Maybe it's your mom, or your coworker that you see every day, or it's your ex and you have joint custody of the kids. What's your advice on dealing with difficult people—being around them, but without letting it upset you?

KATHERINE. First, the practical. Start by limiting the amount of contact you have with them and create inner "policies" that you uphold to protect yourself. That probably seems obvious, but sometimes it's easy to let our boundaries get smushed in without us even noticing. Your policies might be things like, "I don't answer texts from this person after five in the afternoon," or, "We can meet for lunch, but you can't come back to my house," or "I'll show up and be pleasant, but I will only stay for forty-five minutes," or, "Any important correspondence, including anything about dates and times, has to happen over email so there's a record of it." Once you've done what you can in the physical world, you can work on the emotional one. Practice staying in your own body when you're with this person. (This is harder than it seems—difficult people have a way of invading our energetic space and bringing us into theirs!) Imagine a wall of something protective—white light, dragons, flamethrower-wielding warrior goddesses—between you and this person. Say to yourself, "You're safe, you're actually completely safe in this situation," unless, of course, you're not, in which case get the hell out of Dodge. You may find that you can hold on to that pleasantly detached feeling for a certain length of time but that after a while, you still get overwhelmed. It's OK to honor that and keep your exposure as limited as necessary, even if that means saying, "I'm going to have to revisit this. I'll be back in touch later today."

ANDREA. What is your number one piece of advice for setting healthy boundaries in your relationships?

NICK. I feel like knowing your own needs and energy drains are one of the most amazing things we can do for the people we love. If I know exactly what my needs are and the fastest way for me to get them met, then I have the ability to fill those needs with more ease than the person who is just throwing a bunch of things at the self-care wall and seeing what sticks. Since I know what fills my own bucket best (physical touch and quality time) and what matters least (gifts), I can communicate my needs most [effectively] and prioritize my time best. And because I know Katherine's soul vitamins are chunks of solitude and companionable silence, I can make sure that I'm connecting with her in ways that feel good to her but don't really cost me much energy, rather than attempting grand gestures and grand adventures. Knowing what fills you up and what drains your energy and then setting boundaries around those things is the best and trickiest maintenance a relationship can have.

KATHERINE. True intimacy requires two separate people. Collapsing into each other isn't actually intimacy (in spite of every love song you've ever heard). The more you can maintain your own individuality, the more true intimacy is possible—and that's true in all sorts of relationships, not just romantic ones.

Own Your Relationships: Review

1. What are some of the best relationships in your life right now? (Relationships that make you feel happy, energized, supported, like the best version of yourself?)

_____

_____

_____

_____

_____

2. Are there any relationships in your life that are not so great right now? (Difficult situations, tension, festering annoyance, unspoken emotions...?) What could you do to take ownership of the situation and make things better?

_____

_____

_____

_____

_____

3. Is there anything you'd like to change about your online relationships or social media usage? New limits you'd like to set? New policies?

_____

_____

_____

_____

_____

The Keys to Owning Your Relationships

+ Be kind to yourself and others; set healthy boundaries.

+ Practice empathy, even when it's hard.

+ Be willing to take responsibility for your part.

+ Communicate honestly and with integrity.

+ Practice the Four Agreements.

+ If you use social media, don't let it use you. Set limits.

CHAPTER 7

Own Your Past

Inside This Chapter

+ Why it's important to take 100 percent personal responsibility for your biggest victories, as well as for your biggest mistakes.

+ How to view your past in a nonjudgmental light, without shame, and with deep compassion for that younger version of yourself.

+ What it really means to "forgive"—both forgiving other people and forgiving yourself—and why forgiveness is such a gift for your health, your stress levels, and your spirit.

+ How to let things go, once and for all—with no more obsessing, dwelling, or agonizing about the past!

Own All Parts of Yourself—the Light and Dark

The first time I walked into a strip club, I was eighteen years old. I'd met a beautiful girl a few years older than me who told me she worked at one. She was in college and had her own apartment, which seriously impressed me. She moved with confidence, and she had a way of captivating the attention of anyone in the room.

I remember feeling surprised—and kind of special—that she was even giving me the time of day. When she told me she made three hundred dollars cash every night at the strip club, I was stupefied. I was used to making maybe eighty dollars a night at my waitressing job—and that was on a good night. In comparison, three hundred dollars sounded like a massive avalanche of cash.

I was determined to make more money and be financially self-sufficient, and stripping seemed like the pathway to success—at least, it felt like the only viable option for a teenage girl with no degree or professional credentials. I was willing to give it a shot. I drove to a club that was about forty-five minutes away from home, hoping I wouldn't run into anybody I knew—like one of my friends' dads, because *eww*—and I signed up for an "amateur contest" and then asked for a job. They hired me on the spot.

That first night, I had no idea what I was doing. I didn't have the right costumes or the right shoes, and I had no idea how to move onstage without looking like an awkward dork. The more experienced dancers in the dressing room were nice and gave me some pointers. Then, it was time to go onstage.

I heard the DJ call my name—not my real name, my self-appointed "stage name"—and at the sound of his voice, I froze. I was in the dressing room, just a few steps away from the stage, and a voice in my head said, "RUN! Who the fuck are you kidding? You can't do this!" And I almost did run! It was a defining moment. It felt like a coin toss in the air, one of those flashes where my life would be forever changed depending on the choice I made.

Just when I was sure I wouldn't go through with it, my legs carried me onto the stage before my brain had time to ask what the hell I was going to do when I got up there. And just like that, I made my debut as a professional exotic dancer. My performance was anything but smooth that first time, but with some coaching from the experienced dancers, I got a little better the next time, and the next.

Was it a good decision? In some ways, no; but in more ways, yes. I went from making three hundred dollars a night to start to eventually making eight hundred dollars a night. I was very shrewd and entrepreneurial and always sought out better venues with higher earning potential. I was able to buy my own condo at age twenty-two, attend college part-time, and work only six days a month while raising my young son. These were enormous victories for me.

Aside from spiking my income, stripping provided many other rewards. I wasn't just shedding my clothes—I was shedding my fears. With each passing week, my confidence grew. I began to see that people are just people—everyone is human, everyone is flawed, everyone craves attention and affection, and everyone is a total weirdo on some level. After dancing for hundreds, probably thousands of people—men, some women, all ages, all backgrounds—I didn't feel intimidated by anyone. A wealthy businessman, a cute young schoolteacher, an off-duty doctor, the local plumber—ultimately, they're all just people. Everyone is special and nobody is special. This is one of the strange, beautiful contradictions of life—one that I've never forgotten.

Stripping also gave me a space for creativity, self-expression, and artistry. I wasn't the best dancer in the pack—far from it—but I loved planning my routines, my music, my costumes, and my makeup, and expressing myself onstage. It felt so satisfying to put on a jaw-dropping show that ended with applause and a rainstorm of dollar bills on the stage.

And best of all, stripping provided me with a continual stream of immediate gratification. Work a shift. Get cash. Work another shift.

Get more cash. You're not waiting for a biweekly paycheck to hit your bank account. It's payday every day. I will never forget the way it felt to slip into a pair of sweatpants and sneakers at the end of a long night—with a face full of glitter and false eyelashes—and wrap a rubber band around the wad of cash I'd just earned. I'd drop the cash into my purse and feel it *thunk* to the bottom. Best. Feeling. Ever. I'd hit up a fast food joint on my way home, eating salty fries and ketchup, celebrating another victorious night.

I loved having more money and more confidence. But this career had many downsides, too; big ones. For starters, I hated the secrecy. I told my family I was waitressing, because I knew they'd be horrified if they learned the truth. My close friends knew about my work. Some of them didn't approve, some thought it was cool, some said nothing at all. But in most areas of my life, stripping was a secret, not something I discussed. I had to continually invent white lies to cover my tracks. Living that way can be very tiring—almost like having a double identity.

And let's be real: This line of work is not for the faint of heart. Even in the classiest, most upscale clubs, you're going to deal with situations that are icky, lewd, uncomfortable, degrading, and even dangerous. Yes, it's fun to express yourself onstage with your favorite music, bejeweled stiletto heels, and sultry choreography, but there's a seediness underlying everything. I had to grin and bear it (and bare it) every night, even when men spouted degrading comments. I had a roommate—a fellow dancer—who got so burned out on the nightly indignities that she put her cigarette out on a guy's arm after he commented to her that "all strippers are whores." I knew many dancers who succumbed to drug addiction.

One of the girls I worked with, and who had grown up one town over from me, was killed. I was half-awake, blearily feeding my infant son, when I heard the shocking report on the late-night news. She had been found stabbed to death inside her burning apartment.

At another club, I was present at a shooting during my shift one night. I heard what sounded like firecrackers and hit the floor. The shooter had already left the building, but I didn't know that—and I fully expected there to be a psycho roaming through the club with a gun. I was afraid to come out from behind the bar to run to safety. I eventually darted into the bathroom, where most of us hid out until the police came and told us it was safe.

Our boss arrived, and we gathered in the dressing room and huddled around, smoking cigarettes with shaky hands. After making sure we were all OK, we were told, very sternly, "The best thing you can do in a situation like this is keep your mouth shut, and don't say anything." Then we were ushered past the caution tape that surrounded the dark, sobering pool of blood, and we all went home.

I retired from the strip club industry at age twenty-three. By that point, I'd made a lot of money. I'd also spent a lot of money. I'd made some poor investments. I still didn't have a completed college degree. I felt extremely confident in some ways and defeated in others. My stripping career wasn't entirely great, or entirely bad. Like many experiences in life, it wasn't black or white. It was many shades of gray.

Even after retiring, the secrecy continued. For a long time, I felt like I couldn't tell the truth about my past to anybody. Imagine having a five-year block of time that you can't really discuss, or mention on your résumé, or divulge to your family, classmates, or colleagues. It was a bit of a burden to carry. After I spontaneously signed up for a workshop on discovering your Authentic Self—the workshop I described back in Chapter 2—I finally realized that the secrecy and shame had to stop.

I couldn't bear to hide anymore. I didn't want to be ashamed of my past. I couldn't make up fake stories to cover up years of my life. I needed to take ownership of where I'd been—my victories, my mistakes, the light, the dark—all of it. Or I'd never be able to move forward, because I'd always be lugging along a heavy load.

I Am Not a Helpless Victim. (Neither Are You.)

Today, I own that era of my past. I can acknowledge it all—the rewards it brought, the money and confidence it gave to me, and the downsides, too. I don't need to hide it. I don't have to worry, for example, that a journalist covering a story about Barre & Soul will (gasp!) discover that its founder (me) used to work in seedy clubs and then "expose" me. This is public information. It's already out there, because I've put it out there.

But my stripping career wasn't the only piece of my past that I needed to own. There were other choices in my life that haunted me, including having been in a relationship with a batterer who, if I hadn't run to my neighbors' house for help, could have killed me.

I didn't want to own that part of my past. I wanted to ignore it, push it aside, and most of all, blame somebody else for it. But just like the secrecy surrounding my stripping career, one day, I arrived at a point where I couldn't let the issue fester any longer. I needed to own my past—my whole past—including the most painful chapter of all. How did I do this? It all started with a question that I really didn't want to face.

"What Role Did I Play in This Situation?"

This is the question I did not want to answer. After disentangling myself from my violent, abusive ex, there was a period of time—several years—when I blamed him completely. At that point in my life, I saw things in black and white. He was the monster. I was the victim. He was the world's biggest asshole. I was the unlucky recipient of his assholery. Everything that happened in our relationship—the car crash, the fights, the hospital visit, the bitter, painful ending, the financial distress that it caused me—it was all *his fault*, not mine. Or so I told myself.

A few years after that breakup, I attended a personal development seminar that turned out to be one of the most influential weekends of my life. At one point, the instructor told us to make a list of difficult situations that we'd experienced in the past—divorce, bankruptcy, illness, death, dark times. I wrote down "domestic abuse." Then the instructor asked us:

"What role did you play in this situation? What could you take responsibility for?"

At first, I was confused and insulted. "What role did I play? Excuse me?!" I thought to myself. "When there's domestic abuse, it's *never* the victim's fault. How dare you ask such a question? This is so un-feminist!"

I pulled the instructor aside later that day and told him that this particular exercise didn't apply to my situation. But he told me, "Actually, it does."

I was indignant. And then he asked me a series of questions that really challenged and provoked me, the most important one being, "What would it be like if you could give up proving to the world that your abuser was wrong and that you were right?"

That's when I saw how much energy I was still pouring into this event that was supposedly over and in the past. I saw how in holding onto anger and blame, I was actually preventing myself from moving on. I began to see that yes, my ex had behaved terribly, and he'd made mistakes—and I'd made some mistakes, too. In addition to staying in the relationship for the wrong reasons, and ignoring the red flags that came up along the way, I had given control over to him. Checking accounts, credit cards, mortgage payments, vacation plans, dinner dates—I willingly allowed him to handle everything. I gave all of my power away to someone else because I didn't feel like running my own life.

The list goes on and on. No, I didn't assault my ex. But I made other choices—choices that helped to create the terrible situation in which I later found myself. I didn't have to be upset with myself about the choices; just being able to acknowledge them gave me a strange feeling of peace. I started to see that when disastrous things happen, it's rarely just one person's fault. It's usually (not always, but usually) a convergence of several people's choices, including my own.

In the past, I often blamed others for my own unhappiness. But when we assign blame to other people, what we're essentially saying is, "I am just a helpless victim. I am powerless." And that is not true. I am *not* powerless. Neither are you.

When I look back on my past, I no longer think of myself as a victim at the mercy of other people's bad behavior. I think of myself as a flawed human being who made some mistakes, who eventually recognized those mistakes, who escaped an abysmal situation, who learned a ton and grew tremendously, and who is (thank God) doing much better now.

I take responsibility for the part I played in creating my past, the good parts and the bad. I was in charge of my life then—and I still am today. I own my mistakes, just as much as I own my victories and successes. I don't own just "certain parts" of my life. I own it all.

Write & Discuss: Owning Your Past

I invite you to do the same exercise that I did (somewhat unwillingly, at first) all those years ago. Write down some of the most difficult situations you've endured in your life: cheating; heartbreak; divorce; betrayal; financial crisis; injuries; illnesses; or chaotic situations at work—whatever stands out in your mind.

Then write down what role you played in creating that situation. You don't have to show it to anybody, this is just for you. Try to take personal responsibility for the part that you played, however small it may have been, even if it feels uncomfortable to do. (If you were a child when this situation happened, then this exercise will likely not apply. Skip this; there's more for you in the next section.)

_____

_____

_____

Write & Discuss:
Letting Go of Your Victim Story

Did you have any particularly tough memories come up during the last exercise? Did you recall any situations for which you couldn't possibly take responsibility? What if, for example, you were abused as a child? How can you release your abuser from blame when what happened was *obviously* not your fault?

Even if you didn't do anything wrong, it might be helpful to look at your situation through a new lens, seeing yourself as a "survivor" rather than a "victim," seeing other people as "flawed" rather than "evil." Maybe you can see your former abuser as a human being carrying tremendous pain rather than making them a "demon." Consider that someone may have treated them the same way in their childhood, causing psychological damage from which they never recovered. Is there any possible way you can view what happened through a lens of compassion for their troubled state?

See if you can do some writing to shift the story you've been telling yourself. For example, instead of "My dad was an abusive monster..." could you write a new story that begins with, "My dad was a flawed man who suffered tremendously as a child, leading to..." and go from there.

Reframing the Story

Terrible things may have happened to you—things you were too young to control, things that should never, ever have happened. Terrible things may have happened partly because of you, too. But holding on to anger, rage, blame, or feelings of victimization doesn't bring us more power. These feelings just make us feel burdened, exhausted, and often, helpless. That's why it's so powerful to reframe your past in a new light and to tell yourself a new story about what happened.

For example, instead of being a "failed business owner," you can think of yourself as a gutsy person who dared to take risks and who has learned a great deal along the way—hard-won lessons that now, perhaps, you could share with others, or use to propel you to the next level in your own pursuits.

Instead of being a "home-wrecker and a cheater," you can think of yourself as a flawed human being who craves love, sex, touch, intimacy, and affection, like everyone else. You made some choices that, most likely, you will never make again. You've grown, and you're not the same person anymore.

When you reframe your past in a new light, it doesn't mean that what happened was "right." It's simply a tool to help you let go and move on without carrying the pain of the past like a heavy cross upon your shoulders. You are taking responsibility for whatever parts you can while issuing forgiveness to yourself and everyone else who's involved. This is one of the strongest, most life-altering decisions you can make.

> *The weak can never forgive. Forgiveness is the attribute of the strong.*
>
> —Mahatma Gandhi

But Should We Really Forgive Everyone? (Even *That* Person?)

Right now, you might be wondering: *But should we forgive everyone? Who deserves forgiveness, and who doesn't? Should we forgive rapists? Murderers? Bigots? Abusive exes? Military leaders who send drones to bomb soldiers and civilians alike? What about Donald Trump?*

I'm not a spiritual guru. But my personal belief is that forgiveness is always a good idea. Why? Because when we walk around with anger, blame, and resentment, it's like carrying a backpack filled with bricks. It's exhausting. It's distracting. It's difficult to do even the most basic tasks—chatting with your coworker, dressing your kids for school—when you're having continual flashbacks to "that asshole" or "that horrible thing she did" and just how "wrong" it all is.

On NPR, years ago, there was an interview with a Holocaust survivor. This woman got sent to the Nazi concentration camps. She survived. Then she emigrated to another country and started her own business. One night, racist arsonists lit her business on fire, burning it to the ground. She survived, yet again.

The NPR reporter asked how she felt about everything—all the terrible things that had happened. She replied, "I have forgiven everyone. I am not angry." The reporter asked, "But how?" She explained very simply, "My forgiveness is not...for *them*. It's for *me*."

This woman understands that forgiveness is ultimately an act of healing and personal empowerment. When we forgive, we are saying, "I don't want to carry this burden anymore. I choose to let go, to lighten my emotional load, to move on."

Forgiveness doesn't mean that what they did was "OK." Forgiveness doesn't mean that you'll tolerate abuse, disrespect, or bad behavior again—other people's bad behavior, or your own. Forgiveness doesn't mean, "Go ahead, hurt me again! It's fine, really!" That's not what it means to forgive. Forgiveness simply means that you're dropping those bricks. You're saying, "It happened. It's over. I'm not carrying this heavy weight with me any longer." It's a gift from yourself, to yourself—a gift for your mental and physical health, for your stress levels, and for your spirit.

Lily Tomlin wisely said, "Forgiveness means giving up all hope for a better past."

Forgive everyone. Yes, even her. Even him. Even yourself.

Why Do We Do Stupid Things? Usually, Because We're in Pain

Earlier in this book, I mentioned a woman named Nicole Antoinette, host of *Real Talk Radio*. I was honored to be interviewed on the show a few years ago. On another episode, Nicole interviewed a woman named Meadow DeVor. At one point in her past, Meadow was over five hundred thousand dollars in debt. How did this happen? As you can imagine, it didn't happen overnight, and it's a long, complex story.

In the interview, Meadow explains that she had to do a lot of difficult, challenging work: examining her past, taking responsibility for her actions, and asking herself, "Why did I do this? How and why did I create this situation?"

At one point, when Meadow was already in extreme debt, a few wealthy girlfriends invited her to join them on a glamorous vacation. Meadow knew she couldn't really afford it, but she said "Yes" and joined them anyway. The week was filled with drinking, partying, and at one point, a wild shopping spree. Meadow's girlfriends insisted that she buy a ludicrously expensive designer dress. Meadow hesitated, but they insisted. Meadow pulled out her credit card, swiped it, and got the dress—which she didn't even like that much.

Back at home, staring at that dress hanging in her closet, Meadow felt so much shame, and she kept asking herself, "Why? Why did I buy this?"

Eventually, the answer came to her: "Because I was in pain."

Throughout most of her life, Meadow had felt lonely. She'd felt like an outsider, the poor girl from the undesirable part of town with weird hippie parents, left out, not invited to the party, detached from deep, intimate friendships. On a primal level, she just wanted to be liked, loved, and included. That's what motivated her to buy that pricey designer dress: The need to soothe the pain of loneliness.

It's also why she purchased real estate she couldn't really afford. It's why she got into a marriage that wasn't right. As Meadow looked back on her past, over and over, she realized, "I spent that money because I was in pain."

For Meadow, this realization was powerful. It allowed her to regard her younger self with compassion instead of bitterness and shame. She was able to look back on those choices with much more gentleness, reminding herself, "Oh, I did that because I'm a human being and I was in pain. That's why."

I invite you to look at your own past through this lens. Why did you binge-eat every night for an entire year and gain sixty pounds? Because you were in pain. Why did you have sex with that douche-y guy who didn't respect you at all? Because you were in pain. Why did you swipe your credit card all those times you shouldn't have? Because you were in pain.

There are many different kinds of pain—the pain of loneliness; the pain of anger; the pain of resentment; the pain of doubt and insecurity; the pain of disappointment; the pain of feeling unnoticed and invisible; the pain of loss. Like Meadow, try to hold that younger version of yourself—"past you" from a decade ago, a year ago, a week ago, or even twenty-four hours ago—with tenderness and compassion. You were in some type of pain. You acted a certain way because of that pain. You can forgive yourself for what happened, lighten your emotional load, and now, with this new awareness, you can build a completely different future for yourself.

Letting It Go—Once and for All

In Cheryl Strayed's memoir, *Wild*, she tells the story of recovering from a triple-whammy of drug addiction, divorce, and losing her mom (who was only forty-five at the time) to lung cancer. To shed the pain of the past, Cheryl decided to do something slightly insane: hike the entire length of the Pacific Crest Trail—alone. She'd walk thousands of miles: a five month journey up the entire West Coast—and that's if you're hiking quickly—through parched deserts, up and down exhausting mountainous climbs, dodging rattlesnakes and bears.

By the end of the journey, Cheryl is a different person—calmer; more confident; able to reframe the past in a new light; proud of who she is—no longer ashamed. As she completes the final mile of the trek, she's a woman who owns her past, her victories, her mistakes, all of it. She's no longer carrying ten thousand pounds of emotional baggage—anger, resentment, blame, and shame—on her shoulders. She's just carrying a simple backpack with some camping gear, and that's it. She feels lighter, liberated, ready to step into the future. For Cheryl, a massive hike through the wilderness was what she needed to do in order to shed the emotional weight of the past once and for all.

What about you?

What do you need to do?

A pilgrimage on the Pacific Crest Trail might not be necessary or realistic for you. That's not the only way to own your past. You can choose another path, like:

Therapy

Some people opt for therapy, counseling, or hiring a life coach—someone who's trained to listen deeply and help you perceive your past in a new light.

Personal Development Courses

There are lots of great options like spiritual retreats, meditation centers, and yoga teacher trainings that can provide a safe space to heal. I've also found the courses at Landmark Worldwide to be one of my biggest sources of personal growth.

Community

You might want to join a support group where you can tell your story, talk about the parts of your life you want to change, and feel supported, knowing you're not on this journey alone.

Movement

Many studies indicate that physical movement—like thwacking a punching bag at the gym—is one of the all-time best ways to release pent-up emotions like anger and grief. Moving my body in barre class was definitely one of the most powerful positive forces in my life during darker times.

Writing

You can journal; pour out your feelings and write your way into a new story, using the written word to reframe your past in a new light. You've seen numerous writing exercises throughout this book. Flip back through the pages and work through the questions if you haven't done so already.

Rituals

In ancient cultures, rituals were part of everyday life, including rituals for coming of age, rituals for planting new crops, and rituals for death, loss, and letting go. Maybe you'd like to create your own modern-day ritual to help you own your past, shed unnecessary emotional baggage, and step into the future you want. You could write down a story about the person you used to be—an old story—and burn it. You could get a tattoo or piece of jewelry to commemorate a piece of your past that you used to feel ashamed about, but that you've now owned and embraced. Or, as I once did, you could get your friends together and throw an "Ex"orcism Party to celebrate finalizing your divorce or to commemorate all the big changes in your life.

What kind of ritual would feel meaningful for you? Whatever it is, set a date, and do it.

Alexia Vernon | AlexiaVernon.com

She Owns It: Alexia Vernon

Allow me to introduce you to my friend Alexia Vernon, transformational speaker and women's leadership expert, coach, and author of *Step Into Your Moxie*. She has built her career on helping women find their voice and speaking up for women's empowerment.

ANDREA. You've been very open about sharing your childhood experience with sexual abuse and finding the courage to speak up about it. How important has forgiveness been in moving on from that experience, even when you didn't receive the support you expected from some people close to you?

ALEXIA. It took me a long time to recognize that forgiveness was not about letting anyone off the hook for his or her choices; rather, forgiveness was about, as Oprah says, letting go of the hope that the past could have turned out differently. More importantly, it was about me reclaiming the role of protagonist in the story I had created and no longer seeing myself as a victim, rather as somebody who not only survived but was thriving. While that might sound like a strange word to use, I really believe that everything that happens to us, is happening *for* us, even if in the moment it's incredibly difficult. It's bringing us to our knees and forcing us to question everything we thought that we knew about ourselves and our potential.

And so, for me, forgiveness was not something I woke up one day and just did, rather it was a mindset that I wanted to unhook from the cord that was connecting me to my abuser and to other family members who had been complicit in what happened. I wanted to not only cut that cord but free myself from staying stuck in that story, which was inherently disempowering. And it is a choice I have had to make each and every single day when I wake up. I use a mantra, 'I forgive you and I release you' anytime I find myself moving through life and going right back into that old story that somebody—or somebodies—did something to me.

ANDREA. What advice do you have for someone who cannot let go of anger toward someone who has hurt them? What about someone who is haunted by regrets?

ALEXIA. My advice is that we are always entitled to feel the fullest expression of our feelings in any situation. That is part of being a truth teller, not denying what's coming up. And at the same time, I would ask somebody, much like I've asked myself, "How is the way that I'm feeling right now serving me? How is it serving me to live into my fullest potential and to speak my truth to myself and to others?" And if my answer is along the lines of, "The way I'm feeling right now is getting me very much in the way of what I want for myself and what I want for others," then it's an invitation for me to do the work to cut that cord. It's an invitation for me to envision myself sending love to the people who've hurt me, and again reminding myself, "I forgive you, even if I don't forget what happened."

ANDREA. Do you have any favorite books you've found particularly helpful that you'd like to share with readers?

ALEXIA. One of Brené Brown's books, which is called, *I Thought It Was Just Me (But It Isn't): Making the Journey from "What Will People Think?" to "I Am Enough."* I love this book for so many reasons, but particularly because it's one of the first books I've read that really makes clear how common our shame is. It helped me to be able to discern the difference between embarrassment and shame. Embarrassment is, I did something silly or embarrassing. Shame is, I am somebody who is not worthy. That shift for me was a really huge one, in terms of recognizing that my worthiness is not about what I do, it's about the fact that I am human and I'm worthy of love. I am worthy of truth. I am worthy of a friggin' awesome life. And the way she goes into some of the particular forms of shame that so many women carry around with them is just genius, in my humble opinion.

ANDREA. Who are some of your personal heroes (or sheroes)? How have you been able to draw strength or inspiration from their stories?

ALEXIA. My mom is definitely my personal hero, because from the moment I told her that I was being sexually abused by another family member, she changed the course of her life and the course of mine by becoming my fiercest advocate, by believing every word that I said without question, by ensuring that I got into therapy, and ultimately, having to speak up to a lot of other family members who were not as convinced that everything I was saying was true. And I saw her really struggle in a lot of her relationships, being told that she was a liar [and] that she was manipulating me, and her ability to stay strong. [She] never revealed to me until I was much older how difficult of a time she was going through, and she was just such an incredible mom who always encouraged my voice. I'm just so eternally grateful to her for that.

One of my favorite quotes is from Melinda French Gates, who says that, "A woman with a voice is by definition a strong woman, but the search to find that voice can be remarkably difficult." And that was definitely the case for me. I would bet that has been the case for many women around the world, irrespective of the privileges that were or were not afforded to them. But that's the beautiful thing about our voices. They are muscles, and like any muscle, if you want them to be strong, you've got to keep flexing them to buff them up.

Each and every day of our lives we have an opportunity to practice using our voices, sometimes in very little, mundane ways, in terms of setting or rearticulating a boundary, and letting someone know when something doesn't feel right, and certainly in much more significant ways when we speak up and out about issues that are not going the way that we want, or when we speak truth to power, and we call out sexism, racism, or violence that we or somebody we care about might have encountered.

When we unhook from the expectation, [from thinking] that when we use our voice, we're going to achieve a particular outcome, and instead stay focused on using our voice unapologetically in a way that is in alignment with our values, the process gets easier.

Own Your Past: Review

1. What's one of the worst decisions you've ever made? Write it down. Most likely, you made this decision because you were in some type of pain—what was it? What was going on in your life at that time? Write out the story. Then write these powerful words, "I was in pain. I made a poor decision because of that pain. I forgive myself."

_____

_____

2. What's one of the worst things that ever happened to you? Write it down. Can you reframe the story with compassion for the person who hurt you? Were they in pain? Mostly likely, yes. Can you write a few words of forgiveness for that person?

_____

_____

_____

_____

_____

3. Is there anyone else in your life—including yourself—that you need to forgive? What's something "heavy" you've been carrying around that you're ready to release? (A past mistake, a misunderstanding, a grudge?) And how would it feel to have that weight off your back, off your chest, out of your body?

_____

_____

_____

_____

_____

4. Earlier in this chapter, I shared that—for a long time—I was afraid to tell people about my career as a stripper. During—and after—that chapter of my life, I kept it a secret, until eventually it became too painful and exhausting to keep hiding my past.

Is there a big (or small) secret you've been keeping—something you've been afraid to share with other people because you're worried about how they might react? What is it? How would it feel to bring things out into the open, to finally stop hiding?

_____

_____

_____

_____

_____

_____

_____

5. In a few sentences, see if you can sum up the gifts and rewards of your past. For example, because of my past choices and experiences, I've become: _braver, willing to take risks, and empathetic to other people's suffering; and I've found my purpose in life: helping women empower themselves to realize their potential and conquer their goals._

What are the gifts and rewards of your past? What are the qualities you've gained, the lessons you've learned, and the skills you've gained? Write it down. Read it back to yourself. Own the beauty of your past—even the messiest parts.

_____

_____

_____

_____

_____

_____

The Keys to Owning Your Past

+ Make peace with the past by replacing victim stories with more empowering ones.

+ Forgiveness is one of the greatest gifts we can give ourselves.

+ Have compassion for whatever pain was underlying the regrettable choices or hurtful actions taken by yourself and others.

CHAPTER 8

Own Your Legacy

Inside This Chapter

+ Why your legacy is something you choose, not something you find or discover.

+ What the word "legacy" actually means (and why it's not necessarily the same as your job or career).

+ Why sometimes you have to do something "crazy" (change your name, move to a new state, chop off your hair) in order to release the past and move forward with your legacy.

+ How to break out of the "assistant mindset"—constantly helping other people to reach their goals, while ignoring your own.

+ Why it's crucial to start putting your legacy first, not second, third, or thirtieth on your to-do list.

Why Do You Get Out of Bed in the Morning?

Whether we consciously realize it or not, I believe we're all searching for a reason to get out of bed in the morning—a passion, a purpose, some kind of exciting project or goal. What drives you? What excites you? What gets you out of bed? What's the point of your life? Earlier in my life, I didn't have any lofty answers for those questions. What got me out of bed was a toddler in a diaper who would be stage-diving off the kitchen counter if I didn't get up and supervise him. After having my son at age nineteen, I spent my early twenties in survival mode, just trying to earn enough money to feed and clothe us, pay the rent, and slowly work toward a college degree in... something. I wasn't sure what my college major was yet, let alone my purpose! Building a legacy? Not really a priority. I told myself, "I'm still young. I have time to figure out all of that stuff later."

The problem is that "later" creeps up quickly. Before I knew it, I was twenty-five years old, then twenty-eight, then nearing thirty. I began to feel a sense of urgency. "Time's passing so fast. And I still don't really know what excites me, what I want to be doing with my life." It really bothered me. And I became determined to figure it out.

Through a combination of training (barre certification, yoga certification), college (finally having switched my major from English to women's studies after realizing I didn't want to talk about literature, I wanted to talk about the gender politics that burned me up within each piece of literature I read), conversations with friends, conversations with myself, and studying my past and everything I'd survived, I finally got the clarity I'd been seeking.

I want to help empower women and bring about equality for all people.

I want *everyone* to feel powerful and strong. I especially want to inspire women to take ownership of their destinies—to help them see that really, they've been in charge of their lives all along. I want to help women achieve their *"Oh shit, can I seriously do that?"*

goals and get what they want. That is what my life is all about. That is the legacy I'm trying to build.

"But wait a second," you might be thinking. "You run a fitness company. So, isn't 'helping people get healthy and fit' your legacy?"

Not exactly. Even though I run a fitness company, fitness isn't what makes me excited to kick off the covers each morning and plant my feet on the floor. Sure, I'm interested in fitness. Yes, staying fit is important. And yes, I love teaching—or taking—a kick-ass barre or yoga class, because it always feels great. But since the very beginning, my company, Barre & Soul, has never been about abs, legs, and butts—not really. Fitness isn't my legacy. Fitness is just the vehicle—the service I'm offering to my community—but what really excites me is seeing women feel empowered and full of energy, seeing them find community and support in each other and achieve their biggest goals.

At the end of my life, I don't want to be remembered as a woman who was extremely toned and fit or who helped thousands of women tone up their bellies and thighs. I want to be remembered as a woman who inspired other women; a woman who showed others that no matter where you are right now, you can achieve whatever you dream of with enough grit and determination; a woman who helped others see that having what you want in life is your birthright and that you don't need anyone else's permission to go out and get it. That will be my legacy. I'm determined to make it happen.

What about you? How do you want to be remembered by your kids, your friends, and your community? These are the big questions we'll be tackling in this chapter. But first...what is a "legacy," exactly?

What Is a Legacy?

Your legacy is not necessarily your job or the business you run. Your legacy is the ripple effect that you create in the world through your actions, work-related or not. It's the contribution you make. It's how you will be remembered.

RuPaul, who is the most famous drag queen in the world, hosts the Emmy Award-winning reality TV show *RuPaul's Drag Race*. But RuPaul's legacy is bigger than just "hosting an entertaining TV show." RuPaul is building a legacy of tolerance, acceptance, self-love, and love for your fellow human beings. "If you can't love yourself, how in the hell you gonna love somebody else?" RuPaul asks at the end of every episode. "Can I hear *love*? Let me hear you say *love*!" RuPaul exhorts the crowd at the beginning of each finale. RuPaul's legacy is all about love, love, love—love, regardless of your skin color, gender, or how you decide to express yourself. Unconditional love: that is RuPaul's contribution to the world. That's his legacy.

Misty Copeland is making history as the first African American Female Principal Dancer with the American Ballet Theater. At five foot two, she was continually told that she had the "wrong" body type to be a professional ballerina—too short, too muscular, too this, too that. She ignored the critics and cynics and pursued her dreams anyway. Misty is an extraordinary dancer, that's for damn sure. But her legacy is even bigger than that. She's building a legacy of self-belief, trusting in yourself, chasing your boldest dreams, and proving that it's possible to achieve whatever you want, no matter what anyone tells you. That is Misty's contribution to the world.

Nora McInerny had a miscarriage, lost her dad to cancer, and then lost her husband, Aaron, who died from a brain tumor, all within the same year. She took her immense grief and channeled it into several creative projects—like her blog, *My Husband's Tumor,* and her podcast, *Terrible, Thanks for Asking*. As the host of *TTFA,* Nora interviews people who have experienced loss, death, divorce, or crushing professional setbacks to find out how they're coping and what they've learned along the way. It's a show about grief that's surprisingly uplifting and comforting. She's continually reminding her listeners, "Whatever you're going through, you are never alone." Helping people to feel less heartbroken, less alone, less crazy, and more equipped to deal with loss—that is Nora's contribution to the world. That's her legacy.

What will yours be?

Write & Discuss: What If You Don't Know What Your Legacy Should Be?

I once had the privilege of hearing the journalist, former minister, and civil rights activist Shaun King give a talk at Harvard University. Having endured the pain of discrimination many times in his own life, including a beating that would cause him to miss his entire junior year of high school due to medical issues, Shaun's legacy is to tell the stories of present-day racism in America. Every day, he reports the underreported, exposing the systematic racism, including rampant police brutality, which plagues our culture. His legacy is to amplify this issue and not allow it to be swept under the rug.

In the talk I attended, Shaun urged the crowd to "stay bothered." "Your purpose and plan in life is really embedded in what bothers you," he advised. "Be bothered."

If you don't know what your legacy should be, start with Shaun King's advice. Look at what bothers you. Identify something that troubles you deeply, something that breaks your heart, that upsets you, and then dedicate a portion of your life to making that thing better.

What bothers you? Make a list of ten things.

1. _____

2. _____

3. _____

4. _____

5. _____

6. _____

7. _____

8. _____

9. _____

10. _____

Then ten more.

1. _____

2. _____

3. _____

4. _____

5. _____

6. _____

7. _____

8. _____

9. _____

10. _____

Then pick something and get to work making a difference. That's it. That is how you can choose your purpose and start building your legacy. It really is that simple.

Pick Something and Just Begin

Focus. Choose. You don't have to do it all. You don't have to be an animal rights activist *and* a champion for the Black Lives Matter movement *and* bring organic lunches to every public school in America *and* find a cure for cancer *and* fight the obesity epidemic *and* run an award-winning tech company with an all-female staff *and*...you get the idea.

Just pick something—one thing that really bothers you—and funnel your energy into it.

It Doesn't Have to Be "Heavy" and "Serious"

Your legacy doesn't have to be "saving the whales" or "ending sex trafficking." It can be a lighthearted legacy—a legacy of fun, pleasure, spontaneity, delight, and beauty. It can be anything *you* want. This is *your* life.

It could be…

> *It really bothers me that people text constantly and never have real conversations anymore. My legacy is to create a world where people have real conversations.*

> *It really bothers me that women feel unattractive after pregnancy. My legacy is to remind women that they're beautiful in all chapters of their lives.*

> *It really bothers me that there's no healthy salad bar restaurant in my neighborhood. My legacy is to bring a salad place into my 'hood, and by doing that, change this city block and create a ripple effect of health and vitality.*

Pick something. Anything. You don't have to work for the United Nations. You don't have to solve world hunger. Your legacy can be a job, a business, a volunteer project, an art project, a class that you teach, a social media campaign, or a mentorship program that you start or get involved in…just pick something and do it.

Focus on the type of world you want to live in that you want to create, and work to create that world. Take concrete steps to build that world. Nothing feels better than that.

Action Is the Antidote to Despair

Right now, as I complete the final pages of this book, our world feels in some ways like a flaming dumpster fire.

Unchecked police brutality. Terrorists using vehicles to crush civilians. White supremacists marching in the streets. Mass shootings. Political maneuvers aimed to uphold patriarchy. Public debates over sexual assault, prompting survivors to have to explain again and again that their pain and trauma deserve to be acknowledged. A US president filling our newsfeeds with misguided nonsense. Meanwhile, the fight for women's rights and racial equality continues. We still don't have equal pay for equal work, and that's just the beginning. We have so much work to do...

Holy shit, Batman. It's a lot. On days when it feels like just too much, I remind myself of Joan Baez's wisdom: "Action is the antidote to despair." Taking action fills me with hope. Taking action feels like taking the power back into my own hands rather than feeling like a helpless victim. This is what I'm urging you to do, too. Don't be a passive bystander. Take ownership of your legacy. Choose a purpose and live by it.

What will history say about you? What will be said at your funeral? What do you want your legacy to be? What contributions will you make toward creating a better world? No one can make this choice for you. Make it. Own it.

"This is the true joy in life, the being used for a purpose recognized by yourself as a mighty one."
—George Bernard Shaw

Write & Discuss: What Do You Want Your Legacy to Be?

Pick any of the following statements and fill it out. Or discuss with a friend.

I want to inspire people to...

I want to help people to...

_____

_____

_____

I want to teach people how to...

_____

_____

_____

I want to be the first person to...

_____

_____

_____

_____

I want to solve problems like...

_____

_____

_____

_____

_____

I want to wake people up and help them see that...

_____

_____

_____

_____

_____

I want to be remembered as someone who...

_____

_____

_____

_____

_____

My contribution to the world is/will be....

_____

_____

_____

_____

You Can See It. But Will You Build It?

It's one thing to say, "I know what I want my legacy to be." It's another thing to actually *do it.*

What's interfering with your plans? What's slowing you down? Are you distracted, or spread too thin? Are you physically exhausted? Are you feeling intimidated because your legacy is just so big and you don't know where to begin? Are you afraid of failure, public scrutiny, or criticism?

There are so many things that can block us from building our legacies—but every type of interference has a solution. And the solution always comes back to taking ownership of your life—taking personal responsibility to create what you want.

Are you distracted? Then fix that. Take ownership of your time. Start saying "no" nine times more than you say "yes." Declutter your schedule. Delete your social media apps from your phone. Free up mental energy that you can pour into your legacy. You're in charge. You can make these kinds of changes and un-distract yourself. No one is going to do it for you.

Are you exhausted? That's fixable, too. Take ownership of your health. Schedule your workouts and fight like hell to honor those commitments. Make sleep a priority. Forgive and let go. Lighten your emotional load. Dial down your stress levels. As always, you're in charge. You can make these kinds of changes and start feeling better.

Whatever interference you're sensing, there's a solution, and the solution resides within *you.*

The Road into the Future

Below, I've prepared a little guided meditation for you[2]. This works a lot better if you can find a quiet place, close your eyes, and just listen, so I suggest you go to www.andreaisabellelucas.com/bonus and follow along with the audio recording.

Before we get started, a word of advice. We're about to visualize your life ten years in the future. Please don't let yourself get caught up in some of the common pitfalls of this exercise, like feeling as though you have to find the "one perfect answer" to your future, or that you have to know where you'll be in your life, family, or relationships ten years from now. This is all made up! You could do this exercise tomorrow and invent an *entirely* different future. It's all up to you.

Be OK with certain areas of your life looking a bit vague. Maybe you see a partner by your side, but you don't know who that is. Great! This is just a tool to remove any limits on the future you're creating for yourself and to explore what's possible. Have fun!

Visualization Exercise

Picture yourself on an empty road. On both sides of the road are all your present circumstances: your friends, your co-workers, your job, your home, the current political situation, all of it. Take it in for a moment, and give the present a nod of acknowledgment and recognition.

Now imagine looking back at the road behind you. Behind you lies the past: people you used to know, former versions of yourself, historic events, all the way back, even before your life to the beginning of time. Take a moment to appreciate the vastness of it all. Give the past a nod of acknowledgment as well and some gratitude for bringing you to where you are today and for the lessons and opportunities you have received.

---

2 This section is inspired by goal-setting exercises I learned back in the day as a lululemon athletica ambassador, which I've tweaked and adapted over the years.

Now imagine turning to face forward on the road. Ahead of you is the future, stretching all the way out past the horizon, beyond where you can see, even beyond your lifetime. As you walk down the road ahead, you come upon a door. When you get to the door, open it and step through. As you pass through the door, you find yourself in a new space. This space is vast, open and white, like a canvas, holding nothing. The present, the past, and the future are gone. This space is pure potential. It is empty and vibrating with possibility; a space where anything may be called in.

Within this space, we will create a vision for your life ten years in the future. Now don't worry, you can't get this wrong. This is your creation and you can come back and change it anytime. Take the next few moments to notice what you would put there.

Start to ask yourself:

> How old will I be in this future self?
>
> Who and what will I love the most?
>
> How will I contribute to and inspire others?
>
> What will some of my proudest accomplishments be?
>
> What is the legacy I'll be creating, for how I will one day be remembered?
>
> What else would I give to this future version of myself, if I knew I couldn't fail—if anything was available?

Take a deep breath in and out, open your eyes, and sit quietly for a few more breaths.

Now, Reflect

Now it's time to free-write about your vision. What did you see?

_____

_____

_____

_____

_____

_____

_____

_____

_____

What are some goals you might like to pursue? What steps would you need to take to move toward them? What are some actions you could take *immediately* that would get things moving in the right direction?

_____

_____

_____

_____

_____

_____

Dream it, plan it, then do it!

"We don't tell ourselves 'I'm never going to write my symphony.' Instead we say, 'I am going to write my symphony I'm just going to start tomorrow.' "

—Steven Pressfield, *The War of Art*

Do Something Crazy

Sometimes, in order to build the future—and the legacy—that you want, you need to do something slightly crazy; something extreme, or something dramatic. Maybe a demonic exorcism. Maybe changing your name. Maybe moving to a new state. Maybe all of the above. I chose: all of the above.

The year I turned thirty was a year of huge loss and huge growth. A divorce—which had taken years to finalize, with endless court drama, paperwork, and stress—was finally over and done. My BA degree, which I had started and stopped numerous times, was finally complete. And, as I mentioned earlier in this book, this was the same year my dad passed away, marking the end of a difficult, complicated relationship that had consumed much of my emotional energy. In the midst of all this, I'd moved to another state, and I'd moved in and out of new apartments and houses several times.

So many changes, so much reinvention—I had gone through so much, and I definitely wasn't the same person I'd been two or three years earlier. It was the beginning of a completely new chapter: a rebirth. That's when I realized I wanted to change my name.

I didn't want my maiden name—a.k.a., my dad's last name. And I didn't want my ex's last name. It all felt so patriarchal. I didn't want to "belong to" anyone. I wanted *my own name*—one that I chose by myself, for myself. I looked at my mom's side of the family. My maternal grandmother had always been so much fun—my memories of her involved us making up our own music videos and filming them on the camcorder, and her playing the piano and singing loudly over rum and Coke. On her side of the family tree, I found the names Isabelle and Lucas. I loved both. So, I took them and created a new identity for myself: *Andrea Isabelle Lucas.*

It was an unconventional choice, and I had some reservations. I knew it meant I wouldn't have the same last name as my two kids, and I worried this might bother them. Changing my name also felt like a very "diva" thing to do. Would people think I was totally arrogant and full of myself? Would people roll their eyes at me like I was some kind of prima donna? My kids, their friends, their friends' parents, people in our community—what would they think? I had plenty of reasons to hesitate, and yet I knew in my gut, "This change feels right. I'm doing it." So, I did it, and I haven't regretted it for one second.

Changing my name was a symbolic rebirth for me, and it wasn't as complicated as I thought it would be. I filled out some paperwork, wrote a check, and mailed it all off; then pretty soon, I had new documents in the mail with my new name and a fancy gold seal.

After the name change was official, I decided to throw a party at my house—which I jokingly called The "Ex"orcism Party—to celebrate finalizing my divorce and to commemorate all the big changes in my life. I was shedding the past; stepping into the future; and reclaiming ownership of my life—a fresh start.

We made exorcism-themed cocktails and decorated the house in a "purging demons" theme. My new partner's mom brought me a *Merry Ex-mas* cake, which I stabbed with a big knife. You know—good, wholesome fun! I also sold my old wedding ring and spent the money on a fabulous trip to Mexico. So long, suckers!

After changing my name, something shifted in my mind, and I realized, "Hot damn. I can really do whatever I want. My life totally belongs to me." This has been the greatest lesson of my life—realizing that I get to choose what my life looks and feels like—right down to the name on my driver's license. I can take my life in any direction I want. My past doesn't define me. And my legacy can be anything I want it to be.

Write & Discuss: Demon, Begone!

What is something you need to "exorcise" from your life? (An old wedding ring, an old identity, an old job title, an old way of thinking?)

What's something dramatic, even slightly "crazy," that you could do to give yourself a fresh start? (Changing your name, radically decluttering your bedroom, chopping off your hair, throwing an exorcism party, and inviting your closest friends?)

_____

_____

_____

_____

Are You Busy Supporting Someone Else's Legacy... While Ignoring Your Own?

You probably know someone who's a "chronic helper." Maybe your friend is a talented artist, and yet she rarely draws or paints because she's always so busy attending to her kids, her partner, her friends, her nine-to-five job, her volunteer commitments, and so on. Somehow, despite her passion and skill, there's never quite enough time for her artwork. She will happily assist someone else in building *their* legacy or completing one of *their* creative projects. Meanwhile, her own passions get ignored. Julia Cameron, in her iconic book *The Artist's Way*, refers to this role as the "shadow artist."

Or maybe you've got a friend who works as an administrative assistant. She's got plenty of great ideas and goals of her own, but those goals rarely receive her time and attention. Instead, your friend spends more than forty hours a week supporting her boss—helping her boss to achieve her professional goals and helping her boss to build her legacy. Your friend is always helping, supporting, and assisting other people. That's her typical mode of operation. It's where nearly all of her energy goes.

To be clear, I'm not saying you need to run your own company or run for president. Many people are totally happy working behind the scenes (just think of a costume designer, makeup artist, or videographer on a movie set), and many people are totally happy playing a supporting role (like being the Director of Human Resources, not the CEO). That's great! Whatever role feels best, wherever you thrive, do that.

There's nothing wrong with being an "assistant" as your job. What's dangerous is having an "assistant mindset"—chronically helping other people while neglecting your own needs, goals, and dreams. Helping other people is great. But remember that your legacy is the reason you were born. It should occupy the very top position on your to-do list...not the very last spot.

Legacy: First; Everything Else: Second

Far too many people—particularly women—make time for everybody's dreams, wants, and needs except for their own. If your kid needs a ride to the mall, if your partner has an important meeting and needs you to handle carpool or dinner, if your friend needs you to offer a listening ear, you make time for that. But what about yourself? Make sure you're giving yourself—and your legacy—the same time and attention that you generously give to other people.

Sometimes we avoid our legacy because it's too intimidating or too big. It's easier to "busy ourselves" with other projects—a quick burst of satisfaction like answering a few emails, washing dishes, or checking Facebook. This is a dangerous pattern. I don't want to reach the end of my life and realize that I tweeted five thousand times and I answered five hundred thousand emails and, whoops! I was so busy doing all of that, I never got around to releasing this book. Or I never opened a sixth Barre & Soul studio location. Or I never gave a TED Talk about gender equality or facing your fears. And now it's too late. I don't want that to happen for me—or you.

I am begging you, please don't suffocate your legacy under a pillow of administrative minutia. Don't spend the majority of your life engaged in comfortable tasks that feel productive but that ultimately mean nothing, that give you very little satisfaction or pride. Your legacy should be center stage, and everything else is secondary.

Every morning, I encourage you to do something related to your legacy *first*—before doing anything else. For me, what that looked like was sitting down and working on this book for an hour right after my kids left for school and before I started answering emails. It can be one page of writing, or one important phone call, or fifteen minutes of research or studying, or anything you want. The key is to do it *first.*

Get into the habit of making your legacy come first, not last. Don't check texts, don't answer emails, don't cut up carrots for school lunches, don't give away your time to anybody or anything else until you've done something associated with your legacy *first.* Start your day on a purposeful note. Then at the end of the day, you will know, "At least I did that one thing. I made some progress. That counts."

Tabitha St. Bernard-Jacobs | TabithaStBernard.com

She Owns It: Tabitha St. Bernard-Jacobs

Allow me to introduce you to my friend Tabitha St. Bernard-Jacobs, zero waste fashion designer, Youth Director of Women's March, and coordinator of the Empower Coalition. She's a great example of a woman who's building her legacy by speaking up and taking actions consistent with her most deeply held values.

ANDREA. You've dedicated yourself to issues of equality and empowerment, and you had a pivotal role in the Women's March, perhaps the most powerful event I've ever experienced! What inspired the incredible work? Where did it all come from?

TABITHA. The Women's March started with a grandmother from Hawaii, Teresa Shook, and then was propelled forward by a few other cofounders. I came on board a few days after the election. I knew Bob Bland, one of the cofounders, from the fashion world and reached out to her to ask if I could help.

After the election, I felt disheartened and disappointed in the result, but I knew that the real problem was not the manifestation of the ills of America in the form of the election result. It was the emboldenment of racism and white supremacy in the country as a whole and the rights that were now at stake with an administration that does not believe in equity for all. I was driven to get involved because of my son. I knew that I needed to invest all I could toward making this country a safe space for my son. I came to the US from Trinidad when I was nineteen, so it took me a minute to really feel like this country is a place to call home. Having my son really solidified that for me and made me realize that I have an obligation, [both] in the here and now and for his future, to dedicate my life to the pursuit of a better country for him and his generation.

ANDREA. Was there ever a moment in your journey when you thought, "WTF am I doing? This is crazy. I'm not qualified. I can't do this."?

TABITHA. Definitely. I'm a fashion designer by trade. I have two fashion lines. I've been involved in social justice work on a local scale but nothing of this magnitude. In many ways, running my own business is similar to organizing in the social justice space. I don't think, though, that there is a way to be prepared to help organize an international movement. I had moments of self-doubt for sure, but I was inspired by the people I was organizing with to stay focused on the goal of what we were doing. One of my fellow organizers always said that we are the midwives of this movement. We simply helped birth it. That always gave me perspective and helped me realize that we, the organizers, are but a small part. It belongs to the people.

ANDREA. We all want our lives to make a difference, but many of us don't know "how" or "what" to do. Many people feel aimless, like, "I just don't know what my purpose is." What's your advice for someone who feels confused or aimless like that?

TABITHA. If you feel aimless and confused about making a difference, start small. If you're looking to make a difference in your life, start with a small habit and take it one day at a time. I started meditating recently, and I started setting aside just ten minutes a day, and it grew from there. When I miss a day, I don't beat myself up. I just move forward to the next day and start over again. If you're looking to make a difference in your community, start local. Seek out local groups or nonprofit organizations that are in need of help. Most of them are in need of volunteers. You can also start by making a recurring donation to a cause that matters to you. Even if it's twenty dollars per month to a local nonprofit, that could make a huge difference for them and doesn't take that much from you.

ANDREA. Who are your mentors, personal heroes, and people you really admire—and why?

TABITHA. I have so many people I admire! I am lucky to work with people at Women's March that I admire greatly, so I am inspired by them. My mentor and personal hero is my sister Sarah. She's been my mentor since I was a little kid. She's my biggest supporter even in the smallest projects I do. She's the one I call when I'm at my highest and when I'm at my lowest. I admire her immensely. I also greatly admire my husband Adam. He is one of the kindest, most openhearted people I know, and I learn from him every day. I admire Ahed Tamimi, a young Palestinian woman who is constantly under threat because she stands up for her rights and the rights of her family and community. I'm also inspired by all the young people I work with who are using their voices to stand up in the face of injustice. When I was their age, I was not nearly as aware and dedicated to my community, so I'm in awe of all of them.

ANDREA. At your memorial service, which will hopefully be many, many years from now, what are some words you hope are said about you?

TABITHA. At my memorial service, I hope people say that I always tried my best and I was a perpetual learner.

ANDREA. What does the word "legacy" mean for you? Is it something you create, or something you leave behind for future generations? Is it how you'll be remembered?

TABITHA. For me, legacy is very personal. I want my son to be proud to call me his mom. I want him to tell his kids about his mother in a way that makes him happy to have been on this journey with me. My legacy will be in how he remembers me.

Own Your Legacy: Review

1. What is the legacy you are building or that you want to start building?

_____

_____

_____

_____

_____

_____

_____

_____

2. What are some of the different forms that your legacy could take? (A business, a volunteer project, an art project, a book, a blog, a podcast, a new initiative at a local school, or...?)

_____

_____

_____

_____

_____

_____

_____

3. What's getting in the way or slowing you down? What could you do to clear away whatever's interfering with you building your legacy?

_____

_____

_____

_____

_____

_____

_____

_____

4. Cast yourself out ten years in the future. What does your life look like? What have you accomplished? What steps have you taken to build or expand your legacy?

_____

_____

_____

_____

_____

_____

_____

_____

_____

The Keys to Owning Your Legacy

+ Choose a cause larger than yourself and make that your "why."

+ Ask yourself what bothers you the most and use that to help find your purpose.

+ Take actions, but don't obsess, it doesn't have to be perfect. Lots of small actions can add up to a big impact.

Closing Words

This book began with the story of my rock-bottom moment—the night that I checked myself into the ER after being assaulted. It was probably the worst thing I've ever experienced. And yet, I have always felt grateful it happened, because it woke me from my sleepwalking state and made me look closely at the unhappy mess my life had become. It was the moment I finally realized, "Things have gotten completely out of control. I have to take back my power. I have to take ownership of my life."

I began to see that nobody could change my life except for me, and I got to work, taking countless small steps, to build the kind of life I truly wanted. At each point in my story, there was some kind of risk that I needed to take. There were financial risks, emotional risks, and creative risks; whatever size risk I could stomach at the time. Whatever action I could muster—even something as small as printing out my cover letter and résumé and handing it to a hiring manager—I'd force myself to do it. With every risk that I conquered, new possibilities emerged.

So where does this story end? It doesn't. Not yet, anyway. The story is still unfolding. I'm still doing things that scare me just the right amount, like publishing this book.

In the two years since I started writing this book, so much has happened: the Women's March in DC with Carrie and her husband Nate, Crissy, and millions of others around the world who share our passion for equality. I traveled the world with my kids, the way I could only dream about when I was broke. I dropped my son off at college. I found myself on one memorable occasion sharing a stage with Michelle Obama and Billie Jean King to speak about women's leadership. I launched a clothing line. And along with Crissy Trayner, I spent weeks in the English countryside studying with our newfound mentor, Esther Fairfax, whose mother, Lotte Berk, was the original creator of barre.

No, life isn't perfectly neat, pristine, and photogenic all the time. Some things are still messy for me, as they are for many other women, and I've had to continue to fight injustice on both a personal and political level. Still, I feel victorious. Because unlike in the previous era of my life, today, I own it all. I no longer feel like a helpless victim. I can own the situation; I handle it, and I do the work that needs to be done. Some days I might feel defeated and call a coach to talk me out of my negative "why bother?" thought spiral. I'll never be above it all or immune to the blows life periodically deals us.

But I don't feel powerless. I feel powerful. I know what I want my life to mean. I'm not waiting around to be saved. I'm not waiting for anybody's permission. I'm actively building my legacy. Even though life isn't perfect, I know that I am steadily laying the groundwork for how I will be remembered one day, and this makes every day feel important. As I grow older, as I watch my kids grow taller and even watch my oldest go off to college, I feel like time is passing so much faster than ever before. I feel sharply aware every day that we only get one life. In this one precious life, I'm in the driver's seat—always. We can't hand the wheel over to anybody else; it's not their responsibility.

Some would have said that me going from being on food stamps to owning a multimillion-dollar business would be impossible. And it would have been, had I not reclaimed my power. How many "unlikely" dreams and goals do you have in your heart right now? Give yourself five, ten, twenty years and you could be *anywhere*, if you start taking the micro-steps today.

One of my favorite quotes is by the street artist Eddie Colla. He has a piece of art that says, "If you want to achieve greatness, stop asking for permission."

In other words, there's only one person who has the key to unlock your greatness. And that person is you. Call me crazy, but I believe that you and I and every human being on earth are all equally worthy of having our wildest dreams come true. I believe you deserve Oprah-level success, if that's what your heart desires. Oprah

Winfrey was not born with special privileges. In fact, she had to overcome poverty, racism, sexual abuse and teen pregnancy, and look at how much she has accomplished. She never got a notice in the mail from some secret government agency giving her license to do bigger things than most people even dream of. That's silly, because there is no authority who can grant that kind of privilege. She had to give herself permission. And you can do the same.

Your worthiness as a person is not dictated by your past. Your potential doesn't have to be limited by the family or situation you came from, by the choices you made before, or even by the circumstances around you now. No one has a perfect path to success. Those people we follow on social media who we think have it all together? They're just showing us their highlight reel! We know this because we're all doing the same thing, and yet we forget. They're not special. They are dealing with struggles just like you. And if you're waiting for your behind-the-scenes shots to match their highlight reel, you'll never even get started. If you're waiting to be filled with confidence before you begin taking actions, you will never have a chance to gain confidence. Because confidence comes from taking action.

So where do we begin? What do we do?

You don't have to know how to do it all. Just like Alex told me when I was starting my business, you can figure it out. It all starts with one scary little step. Along the way, there will be people in your life who love and support you and who cheer for you, and the more you are willing to reach out to others and share your vision, the sooner you will make that vision come true. But when all is said and done, you're in charge, and nobody can change your life or the world on your behalf. There's no rescue squad, no savior, no Disney prince coming to clean up any of your messes, do your work, or achieve your goals for you. It's all you.

Take everything back into your own hands—every decision. Take back every space on your calendar, everything you are longing to contribute, and everything you must leave behind. Take 100 percent personal responsibility for all of it. Make it happen. Own it all.

Phee Manuel | RomanceAndDance.com |

She Owns It: Phee Manuel

Allow me to introduce you to my friend Phee Manuel, a busy, ambitious woman who "owns it all" like nobody's business. She's got three kids, a pole-dance business called Romance and Dance with three studio locations, the MOST killer sense of style, and a marriage that is #relationshipgoals. She is one of the most straight-shooting, hardest hustling women I know, and she sat down to share a little bit with us about how she does it all.

ANDREA. What gets you out of bed in the morning? What makes you pumped about the work that you do every day?

PHEE. My drive is basically my hustle inside of me. That never goes out. I'm never, ever, ever tired. Especially when it comes to what I do.

ANDREA. So, you hustle your ass off. You get so much done. Can you walk me through what a typical morning looks like for you?

PHEE. When I wake up, I check [daily] numbers, then I also check numbers for the month. I see where I am as far as [the question of] what do I need to do in order to make my numbers better than last month? That's my ultimate goal. And I always have a plan on how I'm going to do that. After that, I check emails. I constantly check emails because our customer service is everything.

After I make sure that all those are done, I check all social media. I got four Facebooks, Twitter, Instagram, Snapchat, I got it all— Pinterest, I got everything. So, I check those and make sure all my DMs are answered, try to make sure that all my comments are answered. After I check that, then I'll get up, go take the kids to school, and take care of the studios.

ANDREA. So, you and your husband are pretty much together throughout the day when you're running all your errands and doing business stuff?

PHEE. Oh, yes. We be together 24/7.

ANDREA. So, you and Bo have been married for eighteen years, and you've worked together side by side every day. What are your secrets for a happy and long-lasting relationship?

PHEE. Don't argue in front of people. If you and your spouse were to argue in front of his friends or your friends, they tend to say stuff that's going to hurt your feelings more, because they don't want to be embarrassed. And learn to disagree. And, shit. Marry your damn best friend.

ANDREA. What advice would you give to women about how to decide which commitments are worth saying yes to?

PHEE. I can only talk about myself. I only say yes to shit that I'm going to get involved in, like, shit that I can commit to. I only say yes to things that I know I want to do. If it's going to make money, I'm saying yes. I'm all in. But I know how to say no. And as far as if I do say yes and it doesn't make sense, I know how to come to you and tell you, "Not no more." It just depends on the situation. For me, my motto is, if it don't make dollars, it don't make sense.

ANDREA. You have an amazing sense of style. Do you have a go-to look for every day? How about for a glam occasion like a big party or an event?

PHEE. My kids, my husband, hate to shop for me. And I don't know why they hate it because I tell them it's very easy. If you look at something and be like, "Who the fuck gonna wear that?" That's me. I will never go into a club or into an event, and you're going to have the same outfit on as me. Never. Never. I just like to be different. I love when all eyes are on me. I'm not basic. I'm that type where, when I walk in, you gonna know it—I'm there. Period.

ANDREA. So many women feel really disconnected from their bodies or their style. They don't feel confident, they don't feel sexy. What advice do you have for women to help them with their confidence?

PHEE. Come pole dance. You'll see a difference. What happens is, with women, when you're young, you basically hear your mom or your dad telling you constantly, "You can be whatever you want to be. You can do this, you can be president, you can be a doctor, you can be a lawyer." But when you get older, who's telling you now? Nobody. You done had kids now, where your main focus is telling your kids that.

When you come to a pole class, that's what we change. We build your confidence because we're that person that's telling you, "You can do it." And then when you *do* do it, you're like, "Shit. I did that." If you want to build your self-confidence, start pole dancing.

ANDREA. What's your favorite thing about what you do?

PHEE. We change you physically and mentally. So, my main thing is when I run into people and they be like, "Oh my God, Phee. I done lost thirty, forty, eighty pounds. Look at me now." And that confidence that they have now is just out the roof. Then you have your husbands that come up to me and be like, "Hey, I love you. You done saved my marriage." With women, *you've* got to know you're beautiful, not just your spouse. You have to know it. So, I get a natural high off of when people tell me what Romance and Dance has done for them.

ANDREA. Can you tell me about a time that you had to forgive yourself or someone else, and then what was it like when you were able to let that go?

PHEE. I basically took a girl under my wing and I showed her everything. Her mother had passed, and I was there for her throughout the whole thing. And then maybe a month later, she was like, "Oh yeah, by the way, I'm opening up a pole dancing studio. And it's only five minutes away from you."

So that hit me hard, because she was like a best friend to me. I would talk to her like thirty times a day. And then she blocked me off of all [her] social media. When I walked through the door for the grand opening, she was like, "Oh my God, I'm so glad you came!" I was like, "Well, why'd you block me and not tell me where the damn grand opening is?" So that hurt me a lot.

And then my husband said, "You better snap out of it, because the only person that can stop this business right here, their last name ends with Manuel. And hers don't. So, get your shit together." So, after that, I had to implement a lot of different things at the studio. For example, if you work for me, you can't start nothing within a fifteen-mile radius, just different things like that. I had to put my foot down on some things. But it wouldn't happen twice.

People are scared [of somebody else] trying to steal their dreams, but they can't. People that try to steal your dreams, they get tired, because it's not something that is their destiny. When I do what I do, I'm going to always outdo you, because I don't never get tired. Because this is what I've been wanting to do for years. It's just like a race. Once you get to that finish line, they'll start getting tired. I'm not that person. I'm that type that at the finish line, I'm going to sprint all the way out.

Ash Ambirge | TheMiddleFingerProject.org

She Owns It: Ash Ambirge

Allow me to introduce you to my friend Ash Ambirge, author, blogger, digital start-up advisor, and founder of the irreverent, longstanding, Webby-award-winning business blog, The Middle Finger Project, making her one of the original gangsters of the internet (a badge she wears proudly...on a pizza-stained T-shirt). She's also the creator of the UNF*CKWITHABLE line of courses and kits for freelancers. Ash has written over seven hundred essays around the web, has been featured in over fifty publications including Forbes, Entrepreneur, and The Huffington Post, and is currently writing a book with Penguin Random House that draws on her working-class past to offer no-BS advice on how anyone can take even the worst of circumstances and turn them around to build the life and career they really want. For ten years and counting, Ash has been on a mission to liberate good fucking people from work that doesn't inspire, from judgey humans with outdated expectations, from roles they're done playing, and from lives they're done living.

ANDREA. You're such a prolific writer, and I know you're very intentional with your time. Can you describe your typical day?

Ash. I do hustle hard and have certain priorities that always come first. For example, when I first wake up in the morning, I have disciplined myself not to look at anything else besides the book I'm writing—no news, no emails, no anything except the book. I won't be showered yet, and I won't answer the phone: the only thing I'll do is make coffee. Then I'll sit for three hours every morning and write. This is when my brain is the most fresh! And it's when I get my best work done. But—and I swear to vodka this is true—I can't do anything else first. I'll get too distracted, and then my brain will go in a hundred different directions, and all of my focus and concentration will be lost. And you need that for the important work! That said, once the writing is done, I'll spend some time reading The Skimm and a couple of blogs I follow, and then I'll get into the rest of my work: managing the team, tweaking email automations, creating new products and workshops. On a good day, I'll stop at around three o'clock and work out; then the rest of the night is mine.

Andrea. What are some things you used to waste a lot of time doing that you don't do anymore?

Ash. Ooh, I used to be obsessive about answering my own email, because I really do want each and every person who takes the time to write in to feel seen. However, this simply isn't the best way to leverage my talents to the max, and it does the business a disservice. My number one job is to protect the business, and chit chatting via email for hours on end is not doing that. So now I've got a great team of gals who engage and make sure that customer service is running smoothly, so I can focus on creating—which is certainly the best way I can help others.

However, the trick was simple: instead of hiring customer service reps, like most people might think to do, I hired creative writers. When you want people to feel seen, you'd better damn well have someone who can write a beautiful email, so this was top priority. There's nothing worse than a cold communicator who seems short and uninterested!

In addition to the gals who help with customer service, I also have a project manager whose title should really be, "Ashley Manager!" She's who organizes all of the moving parts on a daily basis, and then she assigns me tasks in Asana, our project management tool. I cannot tell you how helpful it is, as a big picture idea person, to have someone else you can lock elbows with who is the small details logistics person. She saves me every day from myself!

ANDREA. If you had a whole extra day every week to do anything you want, what would you spend that time doing?

ASH. I'd spend the entire day in bed reading! Especially all of the books that feel like guilty pleasures and not related to what I do professionally.

ANDREA. What advice can you give us on how to stop saying "yes" to too many things?

ASH. Oh, we all do it. But two things have helped me immensely: first, tracking every hour I spend using a killer app called Freckle. I know how much time I've spent on book writing, how much time I've spent on creating every course, and how much time I've spent on something as simple as paying the girls. This helps me realize one very important thing: *everything* takes way longer than you think it will. Being so mindful of how much time goes into everything I do helps me stay realistic and say no more easily.

The second thing I do, however, is keep a really tidy to-do list inside of Asana. You can assign start and end dates and times for each task, and then you can see a calendar that has each of your tasks stretched across days. Once I've got three blocks in any one day? I know that day is out. And that makes it much easier to say no to extra things, because, hey, you physically do not have any more hours in the day. They're already committed.

ANDREA. What is one of the biggest things you've had to forgive someone for, or forgive yourself for? How did you find it in your heart to do that?

Ash. You know, this is deep, but I think the biggest grudge I've ever held was against my parents for dying. They both died when I was young, and I was very angry they didn't try hard enough to help themselves. My mother's death especially could have been prevented. That said, I've also had to forgive myself for the way I behaved when she was going through what she was. I was a teenager, and I was resentful and full of all of these emotions I didn't yet understand, and I remember practically dragging her down the sidewalk into the doctor's office even though she couldn't walk that fast. I'll never forgive myself for that, in fact, but I've long forgiven them both: we are all doing the best that we can, given our circumstances. And in that moment, they were, too.

Andrea. What advice would you give to someone who is haunted by regrets or resentment?

Ash. I've been burned in business a couple of times and had to let that anger go, despite having lost a lot of money, in some cases—and more importantly, a lot of time. And that's precisely what helped me forgive and forget: I don't have time to be angry. We've all got limited head space, and you can't think about multiple things at once, which means that every hour you spend ruminating is an hour of energy you've lost toward doing something wonderful with your life. It's an opportunity cost: you can do whatever you want, but you always have to give something up. I'd rather give up the resentment than the dream.

Andrea. Does writing serve as a kind of therapy for you, and if so, is publishing essential to that process, or do you find that writing solely for yourself is also useful?

Ash. You know what? The more you write, the more you get to know yourself—no matter the forum. I've spent a lot of time writing for the public for my blog, and I've spent just as much time writing in private for a book that no one's seen yet. Both are useful, but there's something to be said about other people seeing your naked thoughts: you try harder to make sense of your experience. It's framed more as a lesson for others, and in viewing it through that lens, you often find that you've learned more than you ever thought.

It's not about telling a story: it's about making that story useful for others. That's been an important part of my own growth as a writer.

ANDREA. What other techniques or processes do you find most helpful for healing emotional wounds?

ASH. One time I took an entire month and went to the woods of Vermont. I spent maybe ten thousand dollars to be there, but I looked at it as a business investment: I needed to get my headspace back. So, I woke up every morning and jogged through the forest. I ate clean food. I gave myself plenty of time to read (yes, in bed!). I allowed myself to exhale. I left Vermont an entirely different person, and now every time I need to heal, I seek solitude.

ANDREA. Any parting words of wisdom?

ASH. Don't wait for an opportunity to be great: go out and make your own. Call the person who knows. Ask for help. Show up for yourself and other people will follow suit.

Esther Fairfax | Lotte-Berk.com

She Owns It: Esther Fairfax

Allow me to introduce you to my friend and mentor Esther Fairfax. After I'd been teaching barre for ten years, I wanted to dive deeper to enhance my studies and go straight to the source; this led me to Hungerford, England, and Esther. Her mother, Lotte Berk, was a modern ballet dancer who fled Nazi Germany to England in the 1940s and then developed the unprecedented method of conditioning and strength training we have come to know as barre—as much a social and emotional experience as it is a fitness regimen. Now in her eighties, Esther still teaches her mother's method. Not only is she an expert in this niche, she is a wise, deeply insightful, and innately playful teacher of many hard-won life lessons on compassion and forgiveness of oneself and others. Her memoir, *My Improper Mother and Me*, recounts with great empathy and kindness the difficult childhood Esther endured as well as the many struggles she faced in later life, including poverty, bulimia, isolation, depression, and a rebirth of personal empowerment in her late forties. She sat down with me to share a bit of wisdom.

ANDREA. How long have you been teaching this method?

ESTHER. Fifty-four years, which amazes me.

ANDREA. Why have you kept up this method for fifty-four years?

ESTHER. I love it. I love the relationship between myself and the students, that we're so engaged. When they go home, they're still in my heart. Of course, because I admire [my mother's] work so much, I want to keep it going and that's what my driver is: don't let it die.

ANDREA. What are the benefits? I hear that there are definite social and emotional benefits of doing this method, and that it's been an important part of your life up to this point.

ESTHER. Yes.

ANDREA. What are the physical benefits?

ESTHER. Do you want me to stand up? [*Laughing*]

ANDREA. [*Laughing*] Yes!

ESTHER. I'm very healthy—*very* healthy. I'm in good shape. I'm frightened to say this. I should be touching wood. Oh, I can touch the bar, because the minute you say that, something will strike you down, not that I'm superstitious, of course, but yes, I don't know how to be quite so comfortable in my body.

That's the funny thing. When we get old, and I'm talking *old*, I'm not talking sixty or seventy, hopefully I'll be like this when I'm ninety, but it'll be thanks to the exercises. Good genes always help, but I've been exercising. Fifty-four years is a long time for the body to always regularly be kept in shape. If you get arthritis, you get arthritis, but if you exercise, you won't feel it. It's things like that. It's not saying it's cured. Nothing may cure you, but you can live with it a lot better so you're comfortable in your body.

Also, of course, I believe you've got to be comfortable in your mind, so issues and problems like that usually are sorted out by the time, I don't know, what age would you say that happens?

ANDREA. I don't know if I've reached that age yet.

ESTHER. No, I don't think you have. I don't. It's amazing because I think I thought I had at your age, and then ten years later, I thought I had, and then ten years after that, I thought I had. Now I know I hadn't.

ANDREA. Maybe ninety?

ESTHER. Maybe. I'll let you know.

ANDREA. What are your proudest accomplishments?

ESTHER. [*Laughing*] Sorry...[*More laughter*] To have left my husband.

ANDREA. It took a long time to get there.

ESTHER. It did indeed. We were together nearly thirty years. It did take a long time. I'm very, very proud, and I've made it on my own, but yes, it certainly is. I'm quite happy that I did the book [*My Improper Mother and Me*], but it's the leaving. It was such an achievement, because he was a nice man and he was a good man. He just wasn't the right man.

ANDREA. What do you yet hope to accomplish?

ESTHER. Well, that's a very interesting one. At eighty-three, I can't imagine that there's anything ahead of me. I keep thinking every morning I wake up, it's like, "I see daylight. I must be alive. I'm so happy." How can I think of a future? I listen to the radio a lot, and there's a program called Obituaries; and I always listen to that, who has died this week and how old they were. I think, "They were only seventy. Oh, my goodness." Sometimes they are in their sixties, and I think, "God, I've added years to my life. I'm so lucky." It's the present that's so important. Whatever happens in the present, I embrace. It's thrilling that I'm here to experience it. I don't know what more, but I'm so open to it. While I'm here, give it to me.

Andrea. If you could have, be, or do anything in the world, what would it be?

Esther. Well, you can't just say one thing—but I will; but there are other things I would love to have done. I'd love to do some research into psychology, what motivates us, how we can, it sounds silly to say, better ourselves, but basically to understand ourselves better and how to manipulate our own minds so we can make better lives for ourselves.

Andrea. What advice would you give to women who are unhappy with themselves that are struggling with body image issues—so, all women?

Esther. That is a huge subject, a huge subject, because they're focusing on the wrong thing, so you have to relocate your focus. If you think about food, that's not the right thing to do. If you think about your shape, what you look like, that's not the right thing to do. You've got to go somewhere else in the mind and work with the mind.

Andrea. Where is that?

Esther. In your thoughts. You have to learn how to believe in yourself [and] talk to yourself. Allow yourself to be your best friend. Would you do this to your best friend? Would you say, "That's a bit fatty here, isn't it? Look at your bottom"? Would you say that to your best friend? Of course you couldn't, and why aren't you your own best friend, I'd ask them. Maybe they'd find answers to a lot of different things.

Acknowledgments

Creating a book turned out to take longer than I initially expected. There were many moments when I thought, "Does anyone really want to hear from me? It's not like I'm Bill Gates or Oprah!" and of course, "I have a hundred other things to do—how am I supposed to fit this in?"

Fortunately, I had a lot of supportive people in my corner who kept encouraging me, nudging things along, and helping to bring this book to completion.

I would love to thank my kids, Roman and Elise, and my partner, Jason. My story wouldn't be my story without you.

Crissy and Carrie, our friendships have truly shaped the adult I've (almost) become.

Thanks to all the Barre & Soul managers, staff, and members for keeping the studios thriving so I could get away with indulging my writing dreams.

Thank you to Mango Publishing for getting excited about this book and taking a chance on me, especially the boss, Chris McKenney, and my editor, Brenda Knight. Thank you to Elina Diaz, Roberto Núñez, Michelle Lewy, Hannah Jorstad Paulsen, Merritt Smail, Ashley Blake, Natasha Vera, and Hugo Villabona for helping to usher this book out of my head and into the hands of readers.

This book would not have been possible without Alex Franzen.

A special thank you for introducing me to Mango.

Thanks to Carrie Tyler, Jen Malone, Tristan Boyer Binns, Linda Sivertsen, and Kelly Diels for being early readers and providing edits, suggestions, insights, and support along the way.

Megan McCulloch, Breana O'Connor, Chris Swainston, Jenna Geissler, and Elina Diaz, thank you for sharing your talents on the book's cover.

Thank you to all my barre mentors who have helped me build the most wonderful career, especially Elisabeth Halfpapp, Fred DeVito, and Esther Fairfax.

Thank you to Allison and Mark Hammond. You were there for me when I needed it most.

Thank you to Don Miguel Ruiz and Amber-Allen Publishing, Inc. for allowing me to share the beautiful Four Agreements.

Thank you to everyone who was interviewed for this book, or whose stories I have shared, including Alexia Vernon, Susan Hyatt, Phee Manuel, Nick North, Katherine North, Sara Mora, Kimmie Smith, Congresswoman Katherine Clark, Tabitha St. Bernard-Jacobs, Esther Fairfax, Margie Altman, Carrie Tyler, and Linda Sivertsen.

Thank you to anyone who has ever worked with those in crisis. There are no words to describe how important you are to us.

And thank you, dearest reader, for allowing me to share my story with you. I can't wait to see where *your* story goes from here.

Own It All: Community

Social

You can follow @andreaisabellelucas and @barresoul on Facebook and Instagram and search for the #OwnItAll hashtag to see book-related photos, videos, and behind-the-scenes action.

Newsletter

You can subscribe to newsletters about feminism, empowerment, fitness and well-being (and all the other topics that I love to write about) over at andreaisabellelucas.com.

Email

Did this book inspire you to charge toward a big goal? To take ownership of your health? To reclaim your time and your schedule? If this book helped you upgrade your life in any way, shape, or form, no matter how small, I would love to hear about it.

You can send an email to hello@andreaisabellelucas.com and tell us how you've taken ownership of your life—and what kinds of changes have been happening for you.

I will try to reply personally if I can (please be patient!) to say "Yeah! Keep going!" or you'll hear from someone else on my team. Either way, we love you, we're proud of you, and we're SO HAPPY this book made a difference in your life.

Own It All: Bonuses

For Your Mind and Body

If you'd like to hear audio recordings that I made just for you, take a free barre class with me, and other goodies, visit andreaisabellelucas.com/bonus

Resources

An unofficial list of cool people and things, in no particular order. For ongoing recommendations, sign up for notes from me at AndreaIsabelleLucas.com.

Books That Have Changed My Life

The War of Art by Steven Pressfield

The Four Agreements by Don Miguel Ruiz

My Improper Mother and Me by Esther Fairfax

Bad Feminist by Roxane Gay

Shrill by Lindy West

The *Harry Potter* audio books by J.K. Rowling, as read by Jim Dale

Breath, Eyes, Memory by Edwidge Danticat

Daring Greatly by Brené Brown (or *any* of her other books)

The 4-Hour Workweek by Timothy Ferriss

Blue Ocean Strategy by W. Chan Kim and Renee Mauborgne

The Easy Way to Control Alcohol by Allen Carr

Sapiens by Yuval Noah Harari

The Artist's Way by Julia Cameron

Things I Couldn't Live Without

The Productivity Planner

Dev 1 Perfume

Rupaul's Drag Race

Asana for managing projects and to-do lists, both individually and with my team

Screen Time (found under "settings") for limiting social media time on the iPhone

Boomerang for Gmail featuring the incredible "Inbox Pause" feature

The Landmark Forum personal development course

A Few Of My Sheroes and Heroes

Esther Fairfax
lotte-berk.com

Shaun King
shaunking.org

Susan Hyatt
shyatt.com

Ash Ambirge
themiddlefingerproject.org

Jessica Valenti
jessicavalenti.com

RuPaul
rupaul.com

Sara Mora
saramora.me

Linda Sivertsen
bookmama.com

Kimmie Smith
sheskimmie.com

Katherine Clark
katherineclark.house.gov

Alexia Vernon
alexiavernon.com

Carrie Tyler
rasamaya.com

Tabitha St. Bernard Jacobs
TabithaStBernard.com

Phee Manuel
romanceanddance.com

Katherine North
declaredominion.com

Nick North
NickNorth.co

Hozier
hozier.com

Maxine Waters
waters.house.gov

Sophia Amoruso
girlboss.com

Margie Altman
margeryaltman.com

Dita Von Teese
dita.net

About the Author

Andrea Isabelle Lucas is the founder of Barre & Soul, a barre and yoga studio with five locations in the Boston area. She's also a mom, a feminist, and a writer who covers topics like gender equality, domestic violence awareness, and women's empowerment. She's been featured in *Forbes, Entrepreneur, HuffPost,* and *xoJane.* As a transformational speaker, she's shared stages with Michelle Obama and Billie Jean King. She holds a BA in women's studies from Lesley University, has studied yoga and barre with some of the best in the world (including Esther Fairfax, daughter of Lotte Berk), practices aerials, and spent time performing in a burlesque circus troupe. You can find Andrea's work at AndreaIsabelleLucas.com and BarreSoul.com.